The
Object-Oriented Approach
Concepts, System Development, and Modeling with UML

John W. Satzinger
Southwest Missouri State University

Tore U. Ørvik
Agder University College
Norway

COURSE
TECHNOLOGY
THOMSON LEARNING

Australia • Canada • Mexico • Singapore • Spain • United Kingdom • United States

The Object-Oriented Approach: Concepts, System Development, and Modeling with UML is published by Course Technology.

Managing Editor	Jennifer Locke
Senior Vice President, Publisher	Kristen Duerr
Production Editor	Debbie Masi
Associate Product Manager	Matthew Van Kirk
Editorial Assistant	Janet Aras
Marketing Manager	Toby Shelton
Text Designer	Gex, Inc.
Cover Designer	Efrat Reis, Abby Scholz

Disclaimer
Course Technology reserves the right to revise this publication and make changes from time to time in its content without notice.

The Web addresses in this book are subject to change from time to time as necessary without notice.

For more information, contact Course Technology, 25 Thomson Place, Boston, MA 02210; or find us on the World Wide Web at *www.course.com*.

For permission to use material from this text or product, contact us by
- Web: www.thomsonrights.com
- Phone: 1-800-730-2214
- Fax: 1-800-730-2215

ISBN 0-619-03390-8

Printed in Canada
8 WC 05

The
Object-Oriented Approach
Concepts, System Development,
and Modeling with UML

Brief Contents

CONTENTS

Chapter 9 An Object-Oriented Analysis Case Study of Dick's
Dive 'n' Thrive 111

Dedication

To Brian, Kevin, and Ida Marie

Preface

It has been a great pleasure to complete this substantially updated edition of The *Object Oriented Approach*. Since the first edition was published, object-orientation has really taken off. The first edition provided a reader-friendly introduction to object-oriented system development for readers with an information systems (IS) interest or background. Based on favorable reviews and extensive positive feedback, it appears to have succeeded in bringing a substantial number of IS faculty and their students up to speed in what can sometimes seem a confusing and overly technical topic.

Many new developments have affected object-oriented development in the last six years. The World Wide Web and the introduction of the Java programming language, for example, have made object-oriented programming a virtual necessity in information systems degree programs. There have also been some important developments in OO modeling and process standards, most notably the adoption of the Unified Modeling Language (UML) by the Object Management Group.

Understanding the object-oriented approach is no longer just an option for those on the cutting edge. But it is still not always clear how to go about learning it. This text assumes that the object-oriented approach and UML are more than just programming issues. For most of us, it takes a major change in our thought processes to truly understand OO. It also remains important to understand OO from the business problem solving perspective. This book, we feel, is just what is needed for most IS students and professionals who want to do it right. The timing was clearly perfect for an updated version of the book.

As before, object-oriented concepts and modeling are emphasized. All examples are now documented and thoroughly explained using UML. Use case diagrams, class diagrams, sequence diagrams, and statecharts are introduced and explained using the same dynamic "object think" approach used in the first edition. Readers will not just learn about UML diagram notation; the book brings the diagrams to life with clear and complete examples.

The book assumes some knowledge of IS concepts, but knowledge of programming (and other technical knowledge) is not required. It is designed for use as a supplement in a variety of IS courses where the instructor wants to introduce object-oriented concepts and methods. It is also quite appropriate for self-study by IS professionals or managers who want an overview of the object-oriented approach without getting bogged down in programming details or the intricacies of a specific development tool.

A common use for this text is in an object-oriented development course that covers object-oriented analysis, design, and programming. This book can be used for the first part of the course: concepts, modeling, and object-oriented analysis and design. The balance of the course can cover object-oriented programming using a specific OO programming language and textbook. With the solid conceptual foundation provided by this book, IS students will be better prepared to learn an object-oriented language like Java, C++, or C#.

▌ Organization

The organization of the book results from our own experiences learning the object-oriented approach. Rather the focusing on definitions at the start, we introduce the object-oriented approach by describing it as a different way of thinking about computer systems. Chapter One discusses the object-oriented approach in comparison to the traditional structured approaches and covers its history, the development of UML, and potential benefits. Chapter Two demonstrates that focusing on objects is a more natural approach for people, and it clarifies the different and sometimes confusing ways people define object-oriented technology. Chapter Three introduces the "object think" approach, which helps people change their thinking to an object-orientation. Chapter Four formally defines the key concepts in the object-oriented approach that have been informally introduced earlier: *object, class, object relationships, methods, encapsulation* or *information hiding, message sending, polymorphism, generalization/specialization hierarchies* and *inheritance*, and *reuse*.

Chapter Five discusses models and modeling in the object-oriented approach, stressing the important UML diagrams and notation. Chapters Six and Seven use the "object think" approach to interpret simple class diagrams, scenarios, and sequence diagrams. Chapter Eight describes object-oriented methodologies and the object-oriented development lifecycle, and Chapter Nine presents a case study that illustrates the object-oriented analysis process (OOA) using a more complex example.

Chapters Ten and Eleven provide an overview of object-oriented design and object-oriented development technology. Chapter Twelve is entirely new—an overview of the Java programming language with clear and complete examples showing how key OO concepts are actually implemented when creating problem domain classes. Finally, Chapter Thirteen discusses approaches for moving to object-oriented development.

■ Teaching Resource Package

The teaching tools that accompany this text offer many options for enhancing your course.

Instructor's Manual with Solutions. The *Instructor's Manual* is available in both electronic and printed formats. This all-new updated *Instructor's Manual* provides valuable chapter overviews; highlights key principles and critical concepts; offers sample syllabi, learning objectives, and discussion topics; and features possible essay topics, further readings or cases, and solutions to all of the end-of-chapter questions and problems as well as suggestions for conducting team activities. Additional end-of-chapter questions are also included, as well as the rationale, methodology, and solutions for each.

Course Test Manager and Testbank. This cutting-edge Windows-based testing software helps design and administer pretests, practice tests, and actual examinations. With *Course Test Manager*, students can randomly generate practice tests that provide immediate on-screen feedback and enable them to create detailed study guides for questions incorrectly answered. On-screen pretests help assess students' skills and plan instruction. *Course Test Manager* can also produce printed tests. In addition, students can take tests at the computer that can be automatically graded and can generate statistical information on students' individual and group performance.

Course Presenter. A CD-ROM–based presentation tool developed in Microsoft PowerPoint, *Course Presenter* offers a wealth of resources for use in the classroom. Instead of using traditional overhead transparencies, *Course Presenter* puts together impressive computer-generated screen shows including graphics and videos. All of the graphics from the book (not including photos) have been included.

Distance Learning. Course Technology is proud to present online courses in WebCT and Blackboard, as well as at MyCourse.com, Course Technology's own course enhancement tool, to provide the most complete and dynamic learning experience possible. When you add online content to one of yoru courses, you're adding a lot: self tests, links, projects, glossaries, and, most of all, a gateway to the twenty-first century's most important information resource. WE hope you will make the most of your course, both online and offline, and please, keep us posted! You can send suggestions to mis@course.com. For more information on how to bring distance learning to your course, contact your local Course Technology representative.

Acknowledgments

Many people helped us with the first edition and with this substantial update. We want to specifically thank John Berardi and James Suleiman for helping us with the first edition. We also want to thank Jim Edwards for his faith in us and Lisa Strite for making the first edition possible. Half of the text for this edition was completed while the authors worked together in Springfield, Missouri (and on Stockton Lake). The second half was completed in Kristiansand, Norway (and off the coast of Lillesand). We thank both Southwest Missouri State University and Adger University College for the use of their facilities and for their support.

Many reviewers provided thoughtful ideas and encouragement on the first edition: William R. Eddins of York College of Pennsylvania; Egil Eik of Agder College; William Friedman of Louisiana Technical University; David Jankowski of California State University, San Marcos; Stephen Lunce of Texas A&M International University; Ronnie Moss of Northwest Missouri State University; William Myers of Belmont Abbey College; and Linda Salchenberger of Loyola University. Their original contributions carry forward to this edition. The reviewers on this edition, Mohamed Khan of Centennial College and Will Smith of Tulsa Community College, also provided helpful insight. We want to thank all reviewers everywhere for contributing so much to books like this. We also want to thank Deborah Masi and the MIS team at Course Technology for shepherding this manuscript so carefully through the production process.

Finally, we want to thank Jennifer Locke for her clear vision and solid support for this project. Jennifer is working tirelessly behind the scenes making a real difference in the way students are learning MIS. Thanks, Jen.

JWS and TUØ

The Object-Oriented "Revolution"

1

Introduction

The object-oriented "revolution" is under way. Information systems managers have learned about the benefits of object-oriented development, they are using object-oriented (OO) development methods and development tools, they are completing object-oriented development projects, and they are looking for people who understand and apply object-oriented concepts and techniques.

It is hard to find a topic related to information systems and information system development where **object-oriented** does not appear: object-oriented programming languages, object-oriented interface generators, object-oriented operating systems, object-oriented database management systems, and object-oriented systems analysis and design.

Object-oriented terms and concepts, such as *object, class, object relationships, methods, encapsulation* or *information hiding, message sending, polymorphism, generalization/specialization hierarchies* and *inheritance,* and *reuse,* appear everywhere in information technology articles and advertisements.

But what is it that makes information technology and information system development object-oriented? After completing this chapter, you should understand what object-oriented means in a very general sense. You should also understand the basic differences between the traditional structured approach to system development and the object-oriented approach. You may also be reassured to learn that, although there are important differences, there are also many concepts and techniques that are similar in the two approaches. Finally, you will know a little bit about the history of and the potential benefits of the object-oriented approach.

What is "Object-Oriented?"

Although there are many unresolved controversies about what makes information technology object-oriented, most would agree that the object-oriented approach is based on a fundamentally different view of computer systems than that found in the traditional structured approach. Some see this as a revolutionary difference; others see it as yet another evolution in information systems development tools and techniques.

With the object-oriented approach, a computer system is viewed as a collection of interacting objects. This means that objects in a computer system, like objects in the world around us, are viewed as things. These things have certain features, or attributes, and they can exhibit certain behaviors. Further, similar things in a computer system can be grouped and classified as a specific type of thing, much as people classify things in the real world. For example, people classify all of the different cars on the road as one type of thing—a car. Types of things can be further grouped into more general classifications, consisting of types of things that are similar to each other in some ways but different in other ways. For example, trucks and cars are both types of motor vehicles.

Another important aspect of the object-oriented approach is that things *interact*, meaning that one thing might do something that affects another thing. People also interact with things. Therefore, people can interact with objects in a computer system, and the objects in a computer system can interact with people. To interact with an object in a computer system, the user simply tells the object to do something, and the object does what is requested. An object can also tell another object to do something—they collaborate to get tasks done. We do not have to know much about how an object works to interact with it, and an object does not have to know much about other objects either. We only need to know what the object does. Then we use it!

To build an information system by using the object-oriented approach, you first identify the objects that are needed in the system. Then in the spirit of "reuse" you try to identify some of the objects that might already exist in other systems, and you include them in your new system, even if you do not know much about how the objects actually work. For objects that are new or unique to your system, you find objects that already exist that are similar to the new objects and you modify them a bit and include them in your new system. It is a building-block approach to systems development.

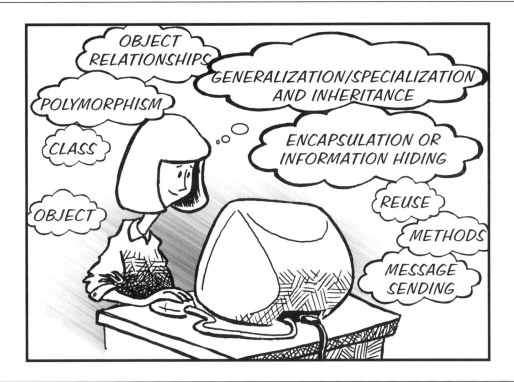

Figure 1.1   Lots of new concepts to think about

If this point of view seems reasonable to you, and if you tend to view a computer system as a collection of interacting objects, congratulations. You are probably in the right place at the right time to personally benefit from the object-oriented "revolution."

On the other hand, if you find this point of view somewhat strange or even illogical, you are in good company. Many experienced and intelligent information system developers have had difficulty understanding and accepting the object-oriented point of view. It is quite different from the traditional view of computer systems. However, most people recognize that it is time to try to "evolve" their thinking about computer systems because the object-oriented approach is rapidly catching on. Fortunately, most of what you already know about computer systems and computer system development can still be quite useful to you, as long as you can begin to change your fundamental point of view. Hopefully this text will help.

How Is the Object-Oriented Approach Different from the Traditional Structured Approach?

Most information system developers are thoroughly schooled in the structured approach to systems and system development. A subtle yet crucial difference with the structured approach is the fundamental view of what makes up a computer system. You might recall how a computer system was probably described in your introductory computer concepts course. Typically, the computer was described as a machine that knows nothing and can do nothing unless given very specific instructions by people.

To make a computer do even the most simple things, specific step-by-step instructions have to be provided by people. The instructions are given in the form of computer programs that have to be very precise and complete, and the programmer has to specify every little procedural detail. Therefore, in the traditional structured approach, a computer system is viewed as a collection of computer programs.

Unfortunately, most people have difficulty thinking in terms of procedural details, particularly when the procedure is complex. As we will discuss in Chapter 2, we more readily think in terms of objects. People with very special talents and skills are required to program computers. Nevertheless, even the most talented and skillful programmers make mistakes when writing procedures. And these mistakes are often very difficult to find and correct.

To make it easier to create logically correct programs, rules for writing procedures were devised that became known as the **structured programming** technique. The structured programming technique limits the programmer to three types of structures, to reduce the chance of logical errors and to make it easier to find and correct any errors. The three structures are a sequence of instructions, a choice whereby one set of instructions or another set of instructions is carried out, and the repetition of a set of instructions.

As programs began to become more complex, additional methods and rules were devised that led to **modular programming** and **structured system design**. Modular programming requires the programmer to write a set of smaller programs instead of one large program, and the smaller programs are organized into a hierarchy, like an organizational chart. The smaller programs are more manageable, and this reduces the complexity of the system. The structured system design technique provides rules and guidelines that help the programmer define how the set of smaller programs should be organized, using a tool called the structure chart.

As computers began to be used to automate a great variety of business applications, techniques for defining more clearly what the computer system needed to accomplish were required. Since computer systems were supposed to solve problems for users, **structured systems analysis** techniques were developed that allowed the systems analyst to specify what processing was required by the users, again by creating a hierarchy of procedures modeled using the data flow diagram. The requirements for the system were decomposed into procedures, using the concept of business events.

The concepts, methods, and tools of structured programming, modular programming, structured systems design, and structured systems analysis clearly focus on procedures and programs. The structured approach clearly views a computer system as a collection of computer programs.

Figure 1.2   Traditional concepts

The Object-Oriented "Revolution"

What is different about the object-oriented approach? The object-oriented approach is based on a view of computer systems that is fundamentally different from that of the structured approach. Once the business events involving the system have been identified, defining what the user requires means defining all of the types of objects that are part of the user's work environment (**object-oriented analysis**). Second, to design a computer system means to define all the additional types of objects involving the user interface and operating environment of the computer system and the ways they interact with objects in the user's work environment (**object-oriented design**). Third, programmers must write statements that define all types of objects, including their attributes and behaviors (**object-oriented programming**). Therefore, in some ways, everything is different with the object-oriented approach.

Figure 1.3   A whole new approach?

Fortunately, the differences between the object-oriented approach and the traditional structured approaches are not so black and white. Many of the same system development concepts and principles apply to both approaches. Most notable is the concept of identifying business events to begin defining user requirements.

Figure 1.4   Most important development concepts still apply when we add in OO

It is also true that the structured approaches have been evolving in the direction of a more object-oriented point of view for quite some time, particularly with the development of data-modeling concepts and techniques. Data models are now universally used in structured systems analysis, and many analysts emphasize the data model much more than the processes or procedures.

Finally, most people (even information system developers) have interacted with some kind of object-oriented computer systems for quite some time as end users of desktop applications with graphical user interfaces (GUI) and Internet Web sites with running applets and scripts. So the object-oriented point of view is familiar in some ways to all of you.

How Has the Object-Oriented Approach Evolved?

The object-oriented approach is not new, although object-oriented development has only recently become more common and influential. The main concepts have been known and used for a relatively long time. The first object-oriented programming language, SIMULA, was developed in Norway in the mid-sixties. The development of the Smalltalk language at Xerox PARC in the seventies introduced the terms "objects" and "object-oriented" in the programming context. Smalltalk was a major step toward making object-oriented development feasible, and Smalltalk was also instrumental in popularizing the graphical user interface (GUI) so widely used today.

In the eighties several existing programming languages were extended to incorporate object-oriented features, leading to C++ and versions of object-oriented Pascal. Additional object-oriented languages were also developed, even COBOL. was enhanced to an OO version in the mid-nineties. In the late eighties and early nineties, graphical user interfaces became increasingly common, and programming packages began to appear that allowed the developer to create user interface objects and a graphical user interface without programming. The rest of the application is then completed using an object-oriented programming language, such as C++.

More recently the Java programming language was developed by Sun Microsystems as a pure object-oriented language that can run under any operating environment, designed specifically for portability on the Internet. Microsoft developed its own version of Java, called J++, and has continued to extend Visual Basic to include more and more object-oriented features.

As object-oriented languages matured, object-oriented development methods began to focus on design issues and object-oriented database management systems (OODBMS). Systems analysis methods appropriate for the object-oriented approach also began to emerge in the early nineties. The focus on design and analysis resulted from the need for a comprehensive approach to developing systems with object-oriented technology.

Current object-oriented development methods use the **Unified Modeling Language (UML)** to define object-oriented constructs and models. Prior to the mid-1990s, a variety of researchers and methodologists developed and advocated their own object-oriented methods and diagramming techniques. Most recognized that some standardization was required in terminology and diagramming notation before the object-oriented approach could become accepted. The UML standard has resulted from the work of many leading researchers and methodologists collaborating through the Object Management Group (OMG) to achieve some standardization. Three key participants behind UML are Ivar Jacobson, Grady Booch, and James Rumbaugh, who now work at Rational Software Corporation, but many other people also contributed significantly to the development of UML.

This book focuses mainly on object-oriented analysis (OOA) and only partially on object-oriented design (OOD). It provides a basic introduction to the object-oriented approach, using the core constructs of the Unified Modeling Language (UML).

▌ What Are the Benefits of the Object-Oriented Approach?

Since the object-oriented approach is increasingly used for developing information systems, there must be some good reasons for this. The object-oriented approach addresses three pervasive problems with traditional system development: *quality*, *productivity*, and *flexibility*. Information systems developed with the traditional approach have been notoriously error-prone, expensive, and inflexible. The object-oriented approach has the potential to reduce errors, reduce costs, and increase flexibility because of its inherent features.

First, each object in a system is relatively small, self-contained, and manageable. This reduces the complexity of system development and can lead to higher-quality systems that are less expensive to build and maintain. Additionally, once an object is defined, implemented, and tested, it can be reused in other systems. *Reuse* can greatly increase productivity, but it also results in improved quality, because the reused objects are proven products. Finally, the system can be modified or enhanced very easily, by changing some types of objects or by adding new types of objects, because the objects are self-contained units that can be changed or replaced without interfering with the rest of the system. These potential benefits are the driving force behind the object-oriented "revolution."

▌ Key Terms

object-oriented	object-oriented programming	structured system analysis
object-oriented analysis	modular programming	structured system design
object-oriented design	structured programming	Unified Modeling Language (UML)

▌ Review Questions

1. What is the object-oriented approach to computer systems?

2. What are the four structured methods that were mentioned?

3. What is different about OOA, OOD, and OOP as compared to the structured methods?

4. How has the object-oriented approach evolved?

5. What is UML?

6. What are the benefits of the object-oriented approach?

Discussion Questions

1. Object-oriented programming languages have been around for over 30 years, about half of the age of computers. Why has it taken so long for the object-oriented approach to gain momentum?

2. From what you might have heard about the object-oriented approach previously, how big of an impact do you believe the object-oriented approach is having on information system development?

3. Why are standards for terminology and diagramming notation as defined by UML so important for the success of the object-oriented approach?

Exercise

1. Find some experienced information system developers and ask them to describe a computer system. Then find some sophisticated desktop computer users, who use spreadsheets, word processing, and graphics, and ask them to describe a computer system. Which group tends to mention things that sound like objects, and which group tends to mention procedures and programs?

References

Booch, G., Rumbaugh, J. and Jacobson, I. *The Unified Modeling Language User Guide.* Reading, Massachusetts: Addison-Wesley, 1999.

Coad, P. North, D. and Mayfield, M. *Object Models: Strategies, Patterns, and Applications* (2nd ed.). New York, New York: Yourdon Press, 1997.

Fowler, M. *UML Distilled* (2nd ed.). Reading, Massachusetts: Addison-Wesley, 2000.

Kruchten, P. *The Rational Unified Process: An Introduction.* Reading, Massachusetts: Addison-Wesley, 1998.

Is Everything an Object?

2

Introduction

To understand the object-oriented approach, it is important to recognize that in some ways, everything can be an object. In this chapter we begin by looking at objects from the perspective of how we learn about concepts and use our knowledge of concepts. We show that the object-oriented approach is a more natural approach for thinking about what we need to know to develop a computer system. We describe a young child, with no knowledge at all, to demonstrate how natural some of the key concepts in the object-oriented approach really are.

Then we focus more directly on objects in computer systems. There are many different types of objects in a computer system, and sometimes it becomes difficult to interpret what someone means when they say they are using object-oriented technology. From this discussion, you should begin to see that everything in a computer system might actually be an object.

Why Focus on Objects?

From a very young age, children develop knowledge about the world around them by identifying and classifying objects and observing the behavior of objects in response to events. Although we do not know how this process actually occurs, for illustrative purposes we will assume it goes something like this:

Almost immediately, a baby begins to recognize a thing later called "mommy." From the baby's perspective, the mommy appears and disappears quite suddenly. It picks up and holds the baby. It provides food. It makes noises. Other things also appear that seem to behave similarly. A "daddy" picks up and holds the baby and feeds it. A "granny" also behaves the same way.

All of these things make funny faces. In fact, it begins to occur to the baby that all of these things have heads, which are always at the top of the thing. These things also seem to have other things attached at their sides, things that grab the baby and hold it. The baby begins to recognize that things are made up of parts, such as a head and arms.

Eventually the baby develops the concept of a "mommy," for lack of a better term. All people the baby sees are classified as "mommies." To the baby, the entire world is made up of only two classes of things: mommies and all other things. All mommies have similar features and behaviors (Figure 2.1). They "have a head" and "have arms." All mommies "move" and "make faces." Some mommies "pick up," "hold," and "feed" the baby.

Before long, the baby recognizes that a daddy and a granny are not really the same as a mommy, although they are all "people." Mommy is a very special class of person. The baby will also learn that there are living things and all kinds of nonliving things. People are classified as a type of living thing. A person might be a big person or a little person (like the baby's brother and sister). A big person might be a mommy person (Figure 2.2).

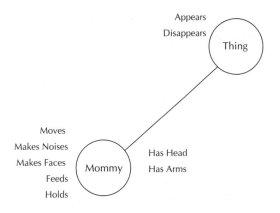

Figure 2.1   Classification of things for the baby

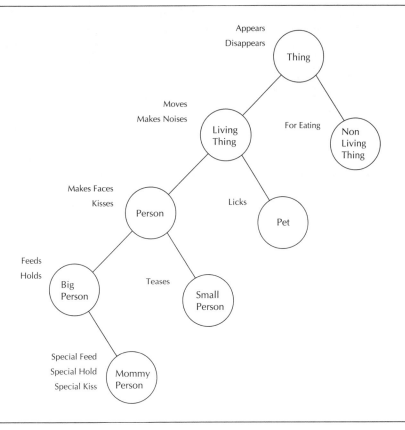

Figure 2.2   A more sophisticated classification resulting in a generalization/specialization hierarchy for the baby

This classification process allows the baby to infer information about newly encountered objects. When Aunt Julie comes to visit, the baby recognizes her as a big person. Therefore, the baby can assume that Aunt Julie will pick it up, hold it, and possibly feed it. The classification process is based on the features and behaviors that make up a class of objects. A more specialized class "inherits" the features and behaviors of all classes above it in a hierarchy. So the baby might assume that Aunt Julie will make funny faces, make noises, and kiss the baby. Finally, as with all things, Aunt Julie will suddenly disappear.

We also begin at a very early age to recognize that things have parts. A mommy has a head and arms. Eventually, the baby realizes that a person, be it a big person, a little person, or a mommy person (Figure 2.2), always has the same parts. Figure 2.3 shows a whole-part structure, which is sometimes called an aggregation hierarchy. The person has a head, which makes faces. The head has ears (to grab), a nose (to pinch), eyes (which blink), and a mouth (which makes noises).

The point of this discussion about the baby is to show that people naturally organize information into classes and hierarchies of general classes and more specialized subclasses—called **generalization/specialization hierarchies**. Features and behaviors of a general class are inferred, or inherited, by specialized subclasses. People also naturally recognize that things can be divided into parts—called **whole-part hierarchies**.

Generalization/specialization hierarchies and whole-part hierarchies allow us to understand things, define things, and communicate about things in terms of other things we know. For example, to define what a mommy is, we might first say, "A mommy *is a* special kind of big person, which *is a* special kind of person, and a person *is a* special kind of living thing." Because of this, the generalization/specialization hierarchy is often described as a series of **is a relationships**. We also understand things, define things, and communicate about things by using the concept of an object and its parts. For example, a person is something with arms to hold you and fingers to tickle you.

The object-oriented approach to computer systems is therefore a more natural approach for people, since we naturally think in terms of objects, and we classify them into hierarchies and divide them into parts. We learn this way, we use our knowledge this way, and we communicate this way.

The object-oriented approach to information systems tries to take advantage of our natural tendencies. For example, if a systems analyst asks an end user to describe what she knows about her work, she might say something like this:

"I process orders, which might be regular orders or special orders, for all customers, both retail and wholesale." (generalization/specialization hierarchies)

"Wholesale customers have many warehouse locations, and each warehouse location has several receiving docks." (whole-part hierarchies)

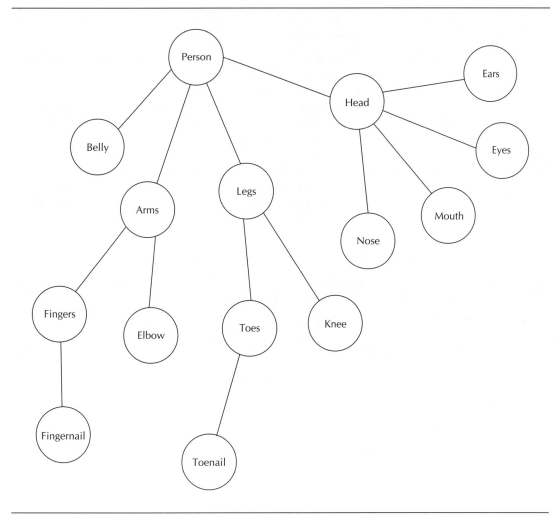

Figure 2.3   A whole-part (or aggregation) hierarchy for the baby

A systems analyst using the structured approach would then say:

"OK, tell me the procedure you follow when you process an order."

A systems analyst using the object-oriented approach, on the other hand, might follow up on the meaning of the objects and the interactions among objects referred to by the end-user:

"Can you tell me more about the difference between a regular order and a special order? Why is it important for you to know about the receiving docks at a customer's warehouse location? When an order is placed, is the customer's warehouse location immediately notified?"

Those of you who are familiar with data-modeling techniques will probably recognize that the approach taken by the object-oriented analyst is somewhat similar to the approach taken when an analyst models data.

Many data-modeling methods are beginning to refer to data entities as **objects**. But as we will see later on, an object is also something more. It has features (attributes) but it also exhibits behaviors. Additionally, the object-oriented approach focuses much more on generalization/specialization hierarchies and whole-part hierarchies, although some advanced data-modeling methods include these structures, too. Finally, the object-oriented approach is much more concerned with the interactions among objects, their roles, and their responsibilities.

What Is an Object?

How do some of the authorities in the field define an object? Coad and Yourdon borrow their definition from the dictionary:

> A person or thing through which action, thought, or feeling is directed. Anything visible or tangible; a material product or substance (Coad & Yourdon, 1991, p. 52)

James Martin defines an object in relation to "concepts":

> From a very early age, we form concepts. Each concept is a particular idea or understanding we have about our world. These concepts allow us to make sense of and reason about the things in our world. These things to which our concepts apply are called objects. (Martin, 1993, p. 17)

Grady Booch uses a variety of approaches:

> A tangible and/or visible thing; something that may be apprehended intellectually; something toward which thought or action is directed. An individual, identifiable item, unit, or entity, either real or abstract, with a well-defined role in the problem domain. Anything with a crisply defined boundary. (Booch, 1994, p. 82)

Others conclude anything can be considered an object:

> An object is a thing that can be distinctly identified. At the appropriate level of abstraction almost anything can be considered to be an object. Thus a specific person, organization, machine, or event can be regarded as an object. (Coleman et al., 1994, p. 13)

All of these definitions acknowledge that an object is something that people think about, identify, act upon, or apply concepts to. And because different people have different perceptions of the same object, what an object is depends upon the point of view of the observer. We describe an object on the basis of the features and behaviors that are important or relevant to us.

For example, a "student" might mean one thing to a professor, but something else to a parent. To the professor, a student is energetic, hard working, and engaging. To a parent, a student might be expensive, indecisive, and lazy! The relevant features and behaviors of an object, to a particular person, is an **abstraction** of the real object. An abstraction can be a simplification of a complex concept, whereby we concentrate only on the features or behaviors that are important to us, or it can be a specialized view of something more general. In either case, an abstraction is specifically tailored to specific needs.

Thus far we have discussed objects and the object-oriented approach. People classify similar objects as a type of thing to categorize them. A type of object is referred to as a **class** for this reason. A general type of thing is a **superclass**, and a special type of thing is a **subclass** in a generalization/specialization hierarchy. When discussing information systems requirements, we are really talking about classes rather than objects. We will discuss this distinction further in Chapter 4.

▮ What Is an Object in a Computer System?

Several authors have attempted to list categories of objects to create a list that might serve as a check list when identifying objects in computer systems. Figure 2.4 shows a classification scheme that combines some of these ideas and adds some of our own. Just about anything that can be considered to be an object can be identified as an object in a computer system. Some of these objects are easy to imagine in a computer, such as a menu or a button. Others might seem more difficult. An airplane in a computer system? A doctor in a computer system? But remember that these are abstractions of the real objects, tailored to the computer system's functions.

Peter Coad uses a concept he calls "object think" to get people to begin thinking in terms of objects in computer systems, because it can seem difficult at first to imagine some real-world objects as objects in computer systems (Coad & Nicola, 1993). Rather than focusing on definitions and lists of categories, Coad proposes that an object simply "knows things" and "knows how to do things." Naturally, most objects in the real world do not really know things or know how to do things in the way that we do, but to help us change to an object-oriented view of computer systems, Coad suggests we try to include the ability to know things and know how to do things in our abstractions of real-world objects. After all, we have reasons for putting objects into computer systems, usually because we need them to know things and to know how to do things. We will use the "object think" approach a lot in this book.

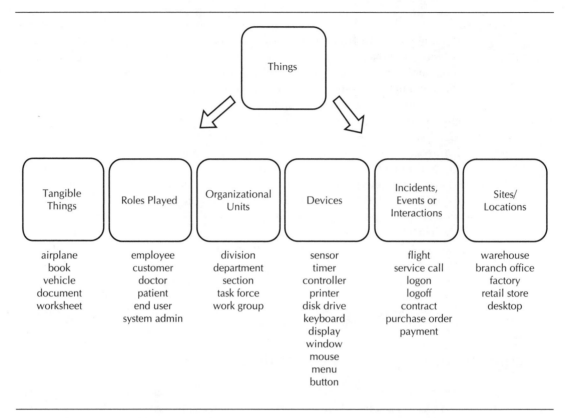

Tangible Things	Roles Played	Organizational Units	Devices	Incidents, Events or Interactions	Sites/ Locations
airplane	employee	division	sensor	flight	warehouse
book	customer	department	timer	service call	branch office
vehicle	doctor	section	controller	logon	factory
document	patient	task force	printer	logoff	retail store
worksheet	end user	work group	disk drive	contract	desktop
	system admin		keyboard	purchase order	
			display	payment	
			window		
			mouse		
			menu		
			button		

Figure 2.4 A generalization/specialization hierarchy of types of objects in computer systems

▉ Types of Objects in Computer Systems

One of the other difficulties people have with the object-oriented approach to computer systems is that the types of objects emphasized differ depending upon the point of view of the developer. If anything can be considered to be an object at some level of abstraction, then anything applying to computer systems can be considered to be an object. That is why, if you look for an article or book about object-oriented technology, it might be about any number of specialized issues. You might be interested in object-oriented analysis, but the article you find discusses network operating systems or client/server architectures.

To help sort this out, we believe it is useful to try to classify objects in computer systems from another point of view. This point of view is based on the type of application or the component of a system that is important to a developer. The types of objects in computer systems might be classified as **user interface objects**, **operating environment objects**, and **task-related objects**. These are defined and discussed below. Some of the objects in computer systems are similar to the real-world objects they represent, making it easier to begin thinking in terms of objects in a computer.

User Interface Objects

User interface objects are objects that physically appear on the computer screen, and end users directly interact with them. They have attributes, they exhibit behaviors, they interact with each other, and most importantly, we interact with them. Recall how we described an object-oriented view of computer systems at the beginning of Chapter 1: a computer system is a collection of interacting objects. Direct manipulation of interface objects by the end user sounds quite "object-oriented."

There are many commonly used interface objects, often called widgets or controls. Figure 2.5 shows some of them, including buttons, scroll bars, text boxes, drop-down lists, check boxes, radio buttons, grids, and others. With visual programming languages, if you want to use a widget or control in your application, you select it and drag it into a window. The control you select is an object that knows things and knows how to do things. For example, a button knows how to be pushed, a check box knows how to be checked and unchecked, a scroll bar knows how to scroll, and a text box knows how to word wrap the text that is typed into it.

When some developers say they are using object-oriented technology to develop systems, they really mean they are using interface objects to develop a graphical user interface for their system. The rest of the system might not be object-oriented at all. Therefore, for some people, object-oriented *means* a graphical user interface.

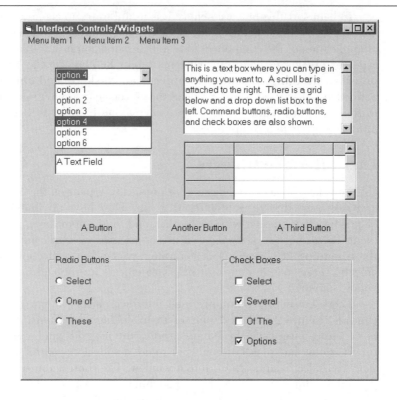

Figure 2.5   Common user interface objects

Operating Environment Objects

Another type of object in a computer system is an **operating environment object**. By this we mean an object that exists somewhere in a computer network or that is controlled by the operating system of a computer. For example, the concepts of a **client** and a **server** in the **client/server architecture** is object-oriented.

A server is an object that provides services for other objects (it knows things and it knows how to do things). A client is an object that requests services from other objects. Examples of servers include file servers, print servers, and database servers. The client is usually an application running on the workstation that the end user interacts with. The end user requests something from the workstation, the workstation does what is asked, and when the workstation needs some help, it might ask a database server or a print server to do something. Client/server architecture sounds just like a system of interacting objects, and that is why, to some developers, object-oriented *means* client/server architecture.

At the level of one workstation, the operating system can be thought of as containing objects. Even with MS-DOS, we manipulate files, directories, and disk drives. By typing a command, we ask a file to copy itself from one directory to another, or we ask a file to delete itself. From the object-oriented point of view, the file knows how to do these things. With most graphical operating systems, we can ask a directory to show its files or hide its files. It knows how to do it. We can drag a file from one directory to another, so a file knows how to be dragged and dropped. We can drag a document icon to a word-processor icon, and the word processor will load the file. We can drag a document icon to a trash can icon, and the document is thrown away. To some developers, particularly those who work on operating systems for the Macintosh and for Windows, object-oriented *means* operating system objects.

Task-Related Objects

Task-related objects are used to actually complete work. These are the "things" that a computer application deals with or creates. These include document objects, multimedia objects, and something usually referred to as **problem domain objects**.

Document objects. Documents are objects that know things and know how to do things. When using a word-processing application, we ask the word-processing document to do all kinds of things for us. First, you ask a document to "open." Then you might ask it to accept some new text, perhaps a few paragraphs. You might ask it to reformat a paragraph or change fonts. You might ask it to cut a section of text and paste it elsewhere. You might ask it to check its spelling. You might ask it to save itself and close itself. The document object "knows" lots of things: its name, its header, its footer, its margins, its font, its text, its number of pages, its author, its date of creation (Figure 2.6).

A worksheet is another type of document object that most end users have interacted with. It knows things and it knows how to do many things too, the most useful being to recalculate! A presentation "slide show" created with a graphics application is another form of document. The document metaphor is widely used for office applications, and the user can now embed document objects created by one application in a document created by another application, such as embedding a worksheet directly in a word-processing document. Groupware, which is an application that supports the work of groups or teams, is often designed around the concept of a document. Most recently, the World Wide Web has been defined and organized as a set of documents. It should be no surprise that to some developers, object-oriented *means* documents.

Multimedia objects. Multimedia systems are another important type of application, which contain sound, images, animation, and video. Multimedia systems also include objects, sometimes called binary large objects, or blobs. For example, a video object knows how to play, pause, freeze, play slow, play fast, or rewind. With a multimedia system, we control the audio or video objects by using interface objects that resemble the buttons on a stereo or VCR.

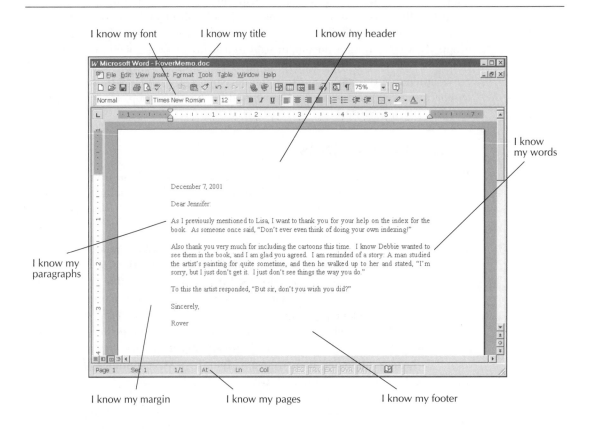

Figure 2.6   A document object

Interacting with multimedia systems should be quite natural for us because the multimedia objects behave the same way as familiar real-world objects. Additionally, we interact with multimedia objects in the computer the same way we interact with the real-world objects. Information systems developers are increasingly being asked to build multimedia applications or to include multimedia in more traditional applications. World Wide Web sites increasingly contain multimedia content. Naturally, to some developers, object-oriented *means* multimedia (Figure 2.7).

Figure 2.7   A multimedia player and a multimedia object

Problem domain objects.   The document objects and multimedia objects discussed above are relatively easy to imagine as objects in a computer system. First, most of you have seen them and interacted with them. Second, they often look like and behave like the real-world objects they represent.

The final type of task-related objects in a computer system is somewhat different. Most people have not (yet) interacted with them, and they (usually) do not look or behave the way their real-world counterparts do. These objects are often called problem domain objects. They are the things typically involved in information processing systems, such as customers, products, orders, or employees. They often correspond to the types of things identified when modeling data, as discussed above. The end user who mentioned customers, warehouse locations, and receiving docks was talking about problem domain objects in the information processing system that supports her work.

Using the "object think" approach, what does a customer in a computer system know, and what does it know how to do? We must remember that the customer object is an abstraction of the real-world customer, tailored to the needs of the end user. Therefore, the customer "knows" things that the end user needs to know about a customer, such as the name and the credit limit. What the customer object knows how to do is also what the end user needs the customer object to be able to do.

Here the "object think" approach is really useful, because the end user doesn't require the customer object to know how to make witty conversation or get up on time in the morning. Rather, the end user needs the customer objects to do things such as create themselves, associate themselves with a new order, change their credit limit, or put themselves on suspension for nonpayment of prior invoices.

Some problem domain objects in a computer system do resemble their real-world counterparts. For example, an airplane in a flight simulator does some of the same things that a real-world airplane does. But most information system developers do not design and build flight simulators; they develop information systems. We are left dealing with problem domain objects that are more difficult to visualize as objects. And, you guessed it, to many information system developers, particularly business systems analysts, object-oriented *means* problem domain objects. This text will emphasize understanding how to identify and model problem domain objects and their interactions.

▌ Key Terms

abstraction	*is a* relationship	subclass
class	multimedia objects	superclass
client	object	task-related objects
client/server architecture	operating environment objects	user interface objects
document object		whole-part hierarchies
generalization/ specialization hierarchies	problem domain objects	
	server	

▌ Review Questions

1. What is a generalization/specialization hierarchy?

2. What is a whole-part hierarchy?

3. What purpose does it serve to classify things and define their parts?

4. What is an object?

5. What are user interface objects?

6. What are operating environment objects?

7. What are problem domain objects?

Discussion Questions

1. Is everything an object?

2. Can anything in a computer system be thought of as an object?

3. Do people more naturally think in terms of objects?

4. Is it really more difficult to think in terms of procedures as compared to thinking in terms of objects? (After deciding, try the last exercise below.)

5. Why does the object-oriented approach mean something different to different groups of people? Is this a sign that the object-oriented approach is pervading everything?

Exercises

1. Assume that you need to explain what a personal computer is. Create a generalization/specialization hierarchy that includes "personal computer," and include all of the more general classes that might be above "personal computer" in the hierarchy. Use your generalization/specialization hierarchy to write a short definition of "personal computer."

2. Create a whole-part hierarchy that shows a personal computer and its parts. Use your whole-part hierarchy to write a short definition of "personal computer."

3. List the "objects" you interact with when getting ready in the morning. Then write a description of the process you follow when you get ready in the morning. Which is more accurate? Which is easier to understand? Which would be easier to redo if you moved to a new house? Which could be more easily "reused" if you were to do the same exercise for getting ready for bed at night?

References

Booch, G. *Object-Oriented Analysis and Design with Applications*. Redwood City, California: Benjamin Cummings, 1994.

Coad, P. and Yourdon, E. *Object-Oriented Analysis (2nd ed)*. Englewood Cliffs, New Jersey: Prentice Hall, 1991.

Coleman, D. et al. *Object-Oriented Development: The Fusion Method*. Englewood Cliffs, New Jersey: Prentice Hall, 1994.

Martin, J. *Principles of Object-Oriented Analysis and Design*. Englewood Cliffs, New Jersey: Prentice Hall, 1993.

3

The Importance of "Object Think"

Introduction

We think it is important to begin believing objects in a computer system are like us: they know things and know how to do things. We need to have faith in them, to rely on them, to trust them. The **"object think"** approach demonstrated in this chapter is very useful for getting people to think this way about objects. After completing this chapter and trying some exercises, you should begin to be more object-oriented in your thinking.

The Need to Change Your Thinking

Why is it important to change our thinking about computer systems? As system developers, we need to begin to accept the fact that we cannot specify every procedural detail in a complex computer system. Therefore, we need to believe objects can take care of the details for us. Ultimately, we need to begin to build information systems by assembling interacting objects that collectively take care of all of the details for us.

We mentioned in the first chapter that understanding the object-oriented approach is sometimes difficult for experienced system developers, but at the same time we described it as a more natural approach for people. If it is so natural, why can it sometimes be so difficult?

Most older (or more experienced) information system developers have thought for a long time that computer systems are collections of computer programs. Since people naturally learn about and think about the world in terms of objects, computer *programs* were the basic building block, the basic object they dealt with. As they learned, they built generalization/specialization hierarchies to arrange everything they knew about computer systems based on this fundamental view: a computer can't do anything without a program.

They also reinforced this view by the way they decomposed a computer system into parts, forming a definition of what they meant by a computer system: a computer system is a collection of programs, a program is a collection of program modules, a program module is a collection of procedures, and a procedure is a collection of very detailed instructions. Naturally, to these people, systems development *means* programs and programming.

To use the object-oriented approach, experienced people have to undo some of this knowledge and rebuild it, but it is difficult for people to change the way they fundamentally view something. So, in many ways, they are quite used to interacting with objects in computer systems, and they can clearly imagine many of the things in a computer system as objects. However, when they switch to thinking about system development, particularly developing systems that contain problem domain objects such as customers, products, and orders (and these are primarily the MIS applications they are paid to build), it becomes somewhat difficult for many people.

Techniques for Changing Your Thinking

There are several widely used techniques that have proven to be successful for getting experienced system developers to change their way of thinking. Two of these techniques are **CRC Cards** and "object think." These techniques are very important for those new to system development, too. The more completely you view computer systems as collections of interacting objects, the more likely it is that you will produce systems that provide the hoped for benefits of the object-oriented approach.

The first technique is called CRC Cards (Beck and Cunningham, 1989), which stands for *class*, *responsibilities* of the class, and *collaborators* with the class. A class is a type or category of object, as we will discuss in Chapter 4. Responsibilities are those things the objects in the class are responsible for doing. Collaborators are the other objects that become involved when an object carries out its responsibilities.

The CRC Cards technique goes something like this. First, a group of people get together to learn more about the object-oriented approach. Index cards are used to represent the classes or types of objects in a system. Each person in the group gets a card and then pretends to be one of the objects represented by the card. They "act" the way their object is supposed to act. The actor playing an object thinks about its roles and responsibilities in the system. The people in the group discuss their responsibilities, as objects, in the first-person. Therefore, they become more used to talking about an object in terms of what it knows and what it knows how to do. Eventually, the group acts out the interactions that are necessary to carry out these responsibilities. For example, for one object to do something, it might have to ask another object to do something first. These are the collaborations.

The CRC technique is more than just an exercise. It is used in object-oriented development to identify and then explore the nature of a required system. It is very useful for facilitating the team approach to development, while focusing on the responsibilities of objects that are emphasized in some analysis and design methods (e.g., Wirfs-Brock et al., 1991).

The other technique, called "object think," is advocated by Peter Coad (Coad and Nicola, 1993), and we use some of the concepts in this book. The purpose of "object think" is the same as CRC Cards, to get people to begin thinking that objects in computer systems know things and know how to do things. The importance of "object think" is the way it begins to change the way people view objects in computer systems *one object at a time*. The "object think" approach is demonstrated in the next section, and it is useful in this book because it does not require working in a group.

"Object Think" for Some Familiar Objects in Computers

The "object think" approach tries to get us to think of an object in a computer system as being more like us. One way to do this is to let the object talk about itself. Once you let the object speak for itself, you will have to begin thinking of it as someone you can trust, as someone who can take care of some details for you. Consider a button that appears on a window in a graphical user interface (GUI). This is what it might say:

I am a button on the screen.

> I know what window I am attached to.
>
> I know my position in the window.
>
> I know my height and width.
>
> I know my background color.
>
> I know what the label that appears on me says.
>
> I know what to do when clicked.

The button knows things (values of attributes), and it knows how to do something (it knows how to be clicked). The button might also know how to do some other things: it can make itself visible or invisible, it can disable itself, and it can be dragged and dropped. We are quite sure every reader has clicked a button or two on the screen of a computer.

What about a window or form in a graphical user interface? Using the "object think" approach:

I am a window.

> I know my title.
>
> I know my height and width.
>
> I know my border type.
>
> I know my background color.
>
> I know what objects are attached to me.
>
> And,
>
> I know how to move.
>
> I know how to resize.
>
> I know how to shrink to an icon.
>
> I know how to open myself.
>
> I know how to close myself.

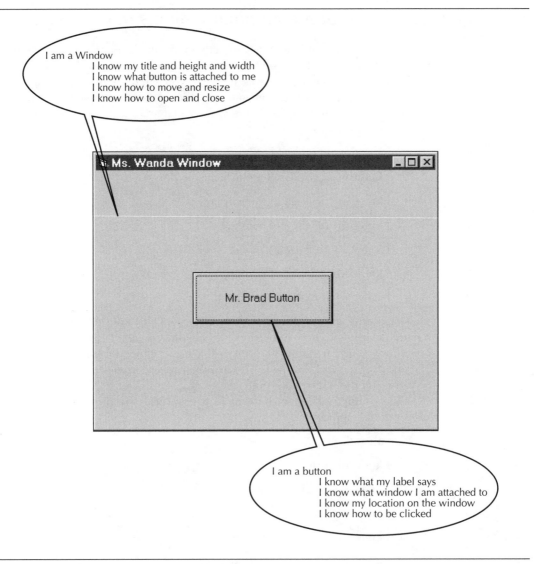

Figure 3.1　What a window and a button "know"

The "object think" approach can also encourage us to think of a worksheet document as something that knows things and knows how to do things:

I am a worksheet.

I know my name.

I know the values and formulas contained in my cells.

And,

I know how to open and close.

I know how to add values and formulas to my cells.

I know how to change values and formulas in my cells.

I know how to recalculate myself.

I know how to insert a new row or column.

I know how to copy or move a row or column.

I know how to sort my rows and columns.

The worksheet knows how to do the things the end user needs it to do. The "object think" approach is helping us define an abstraction of a real-world paper worksheet that is not only like the real thing, but much better. Putting a worksheet object into a computer system creates a very useful system because the worksheet in the computer can do things that the paper worksheet cannot. Once we get more creative about the way we think about objects, we are bound to get more creative about the possibilities for computer systems.

We can carry the "object think" approach a little further by imagining that we can carry on a conversation with an object. Imagine an end user carrying on a conversation with a word-processing document:

OK word-processing document:

Set your left and right margins to 1 inch.

Add page numbers centered at the bottom of your page.

Keep the usual settings for everything else.

Center these words at the top of page 1: My Ideas for the Day

Add a new paragraph, left justified:

Ideas for today are as follows...

Now indent all of the following items, each as an item in a list . . .

Answer my e-mail messages . . .,

Check stock prices . . ., etc.

OK, check the spelling.

Oh, instead of "theere" I meant to say "their." Change it.

Fine, save yourself on drive C: as ideas.doc.

Print a copy of yourself, and then shrink to an icon and take a break.

Figure 3.2   A user interacting with a document object

That was a very one-sided conversation, but isn't that the way you interact with a word-processing document? Perhaps you don't use voice commands (yet), but you do issue commands. When you issue a command for setting the margins, don't you expect that the document knows how to do it? When you issue a command to check the spelling, don't you expect that it will not only do it, but actually do it right? The term "command," which most people readily use when talking about computers, means to tell someone (or something) to do something. Naturally, an object in a computer system knows how to do the things we command it to do (provided we know the valid commands).

Is the end user happy to have a computer system that contains document objects? Certainly! Might the end user describe a word processor as a system that allows her to interact with all of her documents? Most likely!

■ "Object Think" for Problem Domain Objects

The user interface objects and document objects can appear to know things and know how to do things. But consider a class of objects called "dog." We could also think about the dog as an object that knows things and knows how to do things. But what the dog "knows" depends upon the context:

I am actually a dog.

> I know people call me Rover.

> I know people with certain voices and smells regularly feed me.

> I know how to eat, sleep, roll over, bark, and chase cars.

But if we think of a dog object from the perspective of a veterinarian, what the dog object knows and knows how to do are quite different. The veterinarian is interested in dog objects in terms of a *work context*, not the dog's work (barking and chasing cars), but the *veterinarian's administrative work*. The dog is therefore a problem domain object for the veterinarian. To better do her work, the veterinarian might *want* each dog object to know something like this:

I am a dog object in the work context of a veterinarian.

> I know my license number, name, breed, birth date, and weight.

> I know the owner I am associated with.

> I know the check up results I am associated with.

> I know my next appointment date and time.

> I know if my patient status is "all paid up" or "payment overdue."

The dog object that knows these things is not the actual dog, but a dog object in an information system, put there because dogs are part of the problem domain of the veterinarian's work. The veterinarian needs to remember these things about all dogs she treats, and she needs an information system that stores this information. An object-oriented view of her problem domain would reveal that her work system contains a class of objects called dogs. These dogs are abstractions of real-world dogs, tailored to the needs of the veterinarian. What the dog object "knows" are things the veterinarian needs to know. What the dog object knows how to do are things the veterinarian needs to get done.

And what does the veterinarian want each dog object to do? Naturally, each dog object should know how to do things required in her administrative work:

I am a dog object in the work context of a veterinarian.

> I know how to add myself as a patient.

> I know how to tell people information about myself.

I know how to change what I know about my name and weight.

I know how to change my patient status.

I know how to get scheduled for an appointment.

I know how to associate myself with a new owner.

I know how to associate myself with a new checkup result.

There is only one problem: the dog object never said it knew how to bill itself, and billing is very important to the veterinarian. Using the "object think" approach, the dog object has been asked to do something that it does not know how to do:

I am a dog object in the work context of a veterinarian.

Someone just asked me to bill myself.

But I don't know how to do that!

So the veterinarian must handle this chore. The veterinarian probably needs an owner object in her system, too. The owner object can be responsible for billing the real owner, and the dog object can be responsible for telling the owner object when to do it. If the veterinarian had a system that contained dog objects and owner objects, she would really be happy.

It takes some practice to get the hang of "object think." Consider another example. This time the real-world object knows absolutely nothing:

I am actually a rock.

I don't know anything.

I don't know how to do anything.

But if we think of a rock from the perspective of a rock collector, what the rock knows and knows how to do might be something like this:

I am a rock in the work context of a rock collector.

I know my type, weight, shape, color, density, and appraised value.

I know who found me.

I know where I was found.

I know when I was found.

And,

I know how to tell people information about myself.

I know how to add myself to a collection.

I know how to associate myself with a shelf.

I know how to remove myself from a collection.

The *work context*, from the perspective of the rock collector, is to get new rocks, add them to a collection, and keep information about the rocks that visitors might be interested in. An information system containing a class of objects named rock would be able to handle these tasks for the rock collector. The rock collector would be very happy with an information system that contained rock objects.

We have used the "object think" approach to begin describing objects in computer systems. "Object think," and other techniques such as CRC Cards, helps get people thinking that objects in computer systems know things and know how to do things. The user interface objects and document objects described using "object think" are probably easy to accept. The problem domain objects in our examples can seem a bit strange when we use "object think," but even if the technique might seem a little strange, or even silly, it is very useful.

The problem domain objects in our examples are in some ways similar to the data entities identified when a systems analyst models data. Most information system developers are fairly comfortable with problem domain data entities. Hopefully, though, the "object think" approach reveals an important difference: objects can do things and they can interact with users and other objects. What the objects know how to do becomes very important when defining the requirements for a computer system that makes work easier (or more effective) for the end user. The "object think" approach really helps to get people thinking in terms of object-oriented systems.

▌ Key Terms

CRC cards
"object think"

▌ Review Questions

1. Why is the object-oriented approach sometimes difficult for experienced system developers?

2. What are two techniques for changing people's thinking about objects?

3. What does the "object think" technique encourage people to think objects are like?

4. What two capabilities can you assume objects have?

Discussion Question

1. Discuss whether the object-oriented approach is:
    a. easy or difficult
    b. natural or unnatural
    c. radical change or evolutionary change

Exercises

1. Identify and name the following objects and identify their work context based on the "object think" description provided:

    I am a(n) _____ in the work context of a(n) _____.

    I know my title, author, and call number.

    And,

    I know how to be checked out.

    I know how to be returned.

    I am a(n) _____ in the work context of a(n) _____.

    I know my title, author, publisher, price, and ISBN number.

    And,

    I know how to be put on order.

    I know how to be stocked.

    I know how to be sold.

    I know how to be returned.

2. Use the "object think" approach to write descriptions of the following. Let the object speak for itself.
    a. I am an actual tree.
    b. I am a tree object in the work context of a lumber company.
    c. I am a tree object in the work context of a landscape architect.

3. Use the "object think" approach to write descriptions of the following. Let the object speak for itself.
    a. I am an actual car.
    b. I am a car object in the work context of a repair shop.
    c. I am a car object in the work context of a car collector.

References

Beck, K. and Cunningham, W. "A laboratory for teaching object-oriented thinking," *Proceedings of the 1989 OOPSLA Conference on Objected-Oriented Programming Systems, Languages, and Applications.* New York, New York: ACM, 1989, pp. 1–6.

Coad, P. and Nicola. *Object-Oriented Programming.* Englewood Cliffs, New Jersey: Prentice Hall, 1993.

Wirfs-Brock, R. et al. *Designing Object-Oriented Software.* Englewood Cliffs, New Jersey: Prentice Hall, 1990.

4

Basic Object-Oriented Concepts

Introduction

In this chapter, we define and describe the important concepts and terms that are used with the object-oriented approach. Many of the concepts were introduced in Chapters 2 and 3, but the emphasis there was on understanding what the object-oriented approach is like. Now we can more formally discuss these terms, and hopefully the definitions will be clearer now that you have been thinking about objects and what they are. After completing this chapter you should understand all of the following object-oriented concepts: *object, class, attributes of a class, association relationships, whole-part relationships, methods or operations, encapsulation* or *information hiding, message sending, polymorphism, generalization/specialization hierarchies* and *inheritance,* and *reuse.*

A Class Versus an Object

In Chapter 2, we discussed how people classify objects. For example, the mommy, the daddy, and the granny were classified as big people. In Chapter 3, Rover and others treated by the veterinarian could be classified as dogs. Rock number 134, rock number 332, and rock number 607 can be classified as rocks.

A **class** is therefore a *type* of thing, and all specific things that fit the general definition of the class are things that belong to the class. The doctor, Rover, and rock number 607 are specific things, and in a specific context each of these is an object that belongs to a class. Each of these objects belongs to a different class.

When we described objects in a work context (like the dog or the rock), we were talking about objects, but we really meant classes of objects. A class is much like the data entity type used when modeling data. A data entity type is a general category of data, and an instance of an entity type is data about one specific thing. For example, a customer is the data entity type, and Acme Construction is one specific customer. Therefore, a *class* is the general category, and an *object* is a specific instance.

Each object in a class should be identifiable in some way so we can tell which object is which. Usually one attribute, or piece of information about an object, is used to identify an object in the user's work context. When modeling data, an identifier is also required. Sometimes the object naturally has an identifier, such as the Social Security number for a person or the name for a state. Other times the identifier must be created by the system to allow an object to be uniquely identified.

An object in a computer system has an additional identifier called an **object reference**. The computer creates an object reference for each object when the object is created, and any time a message is sent to the object, the object reference is used as an address.

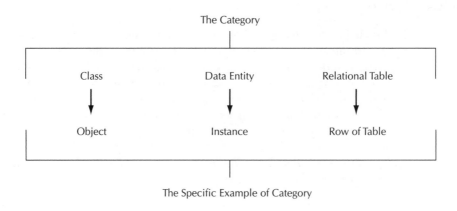

The Category

Class   Data Entity   Relational Table

Object   Instance   Row of Table

The Specific Example of Category

Figure 4.1   Classes, data entities, and relational tables

The other types of objects in the information systems described in Chapter 2 are also really classes. For example, the interface objects—a button and a window—were specific things, but the button object belongs to a class named Button, and the window object belongs to a class named Window. All button objects have the same attributes and behaviors. All window objects have the same attributes and behaviors. When we interact with a specific window, we are interacting with an object. But when we talk about windows generally, we are talking about a class. The operating environment objects discussed are also really classes. Understanding the distinction between a class and an object is very important.

Attributes of a Class

A class of objects is often defined on the basis of the attributes that all of the objects in the class share. All dogs have a name and a breed, for example. As we mentioned previously, an **attribute** is one piece of information that needs to be known about the objects in the class. Each object might have a different value for the attribute. One dog is named Rover, and the other is named Smiley.

The attribute values are part of what an object "knows" when you use the "object think" approach. A dog object knows its name, for example. The list of attributes that applies to a class is what the class of objects "knows." For example, the dog class knows that it has the attributes name and breed. When the dog class creates a new dog object, it knows it needs values for these attributes.

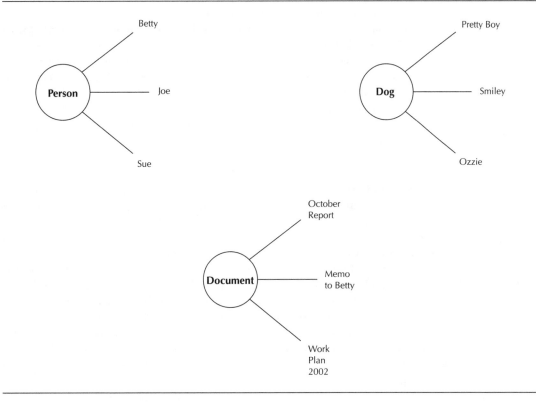

Figure 4.2   Classes and objects

Attributes of a class of objects are equivalent to attributes of a data entity type. There is really nothing new here for those who are familiar with data modeling, so an attribute can also be one of several data types. For example, the dog's breed might be character data, but the dog's age might be numeric. Classes of objects increasingly include newer data types, such as a bitmap of a picture, sound, or even video.

▌ Object Relationships

An object might also be naturally related to other objects. **Object relationships** are much like relationships in a data model. A relationship is an association based on the context in which we view the objects. For example, a dog might be associated with an owner in the work context of the veterinarian. An owner might be associated with many dogs. Similarly, a rock might be associated with one shelf, and a shelf might be associated with many rocks.

With the "object think" approach an object knows about other objects it is associated with or connected to. If a dog object is associated with an owner object, the dog object knows about its owner.

User interface objects can also be associated with other objects. For example, a button might be attached to a window, and each window might have many buttons attached to it. A menu might contain many menu items, and each menu item might be contained on one menu.

As with relationships in a data model, object relationships are usually named or described in two directions. This is done because there are really two relationships, and the name given to each relationship is very important for making the nature of the relationship clear. Each direction of a relationship can be read like a sentence, in the form of a noun-verb-noun phrase, such as "a rock is associated with one shelf" and "a shelf is associated with many rocks."

The nature of an object relationship can also be described very precisely, just as in data modeling. For example, a relationship can be optional or mandatory. An optional relationship means that an object might be associated with another object, such as "a rock might be associated with one shelf." In the rock museum, a rock might not be on a shelf, even though most are. A mandatory relationship means that an association must exist. When modeling data, rules usually define whether a relationship is mandatory or optional, and these rules can apply to objects in the same way.

The other aspect of an object relationship that is the same as in data modeling is the cardinality of a relationship. **Cardinality** refers to the number of associations that naturally occur between objects. The Unified Modeling Language (UML) uses the term **multiplicity** in place of cardinality. For example, a dog is owned by one and only one owner. This is a one-to-one relationship. On the other hand, an owner might own many dogs. This is a one-to-many relationship. When modeling data, beginners are often tempted to say the relationship between owners and dogs is one to many. But actually, there are two relationships. Dog to owner is one to one and owner to dog is one to many. Finally, a relationship can be many to many. Many-to-many relationships are really two separate one-to-many relationships when you read the relationship from each direction. For example, a student is enrolled in many classes, and a class contains many students.

Object relationships, like relationships in data modeling, can become quite complex, because there are many special cases that can occur. To address more complex relationships, we suggest that you familiarize yourself with advanced, special cases, such as recursive relationships, associative relationships, and three- or even four-way relationships. Since this book is an introduction to object-oriented concepts, we will not describe these advanced issues in object relationships.

There are two types of object relationships of concern here: **association** (or connection) **relationships** just described and **whole-part relationships**. An association relationship means that one object is naturally associated with other objects in some way. A whole-part relationship means that the relationship between objects is stronger. There are actually two types of whole-part relationships: **aggregation relationships** and **composition relationships**, with composition being the strongest association.

Whole-part hierarchies, as discussed in Chapter 2, imply that there are strong relationships between an object and other objects that are really its parts, so the whole-part relationship can be viewed as a special type of association relationship. Many of the examples above are actually whole-part relationships. For example, a shelf contains many rocks, and the rocks on the shelf have a strong, and even physical, relationship with the shelf. They are part of the shelf. Similarly, a button is part of a window. A window might have many different types of parts. It might have three buttons, one text box, and seven labels. Mandatory versus optional relationships and cardinality also apply to whole-part relationships.

We believe the distinction between an association (or connection) relationship and a whole-part relationship is not crucial for understanding the object-oriented approach. But since it is often useful to define objects in terms of their parts, particularly when users view their problem domain this way, we include examples of whole-part relationships (aggregation and composition) in Chapter 7.

Methods or Operations of a Class

Classes versus objects, attributes of classes of objects, and relationships among objects should be familiar concepts for those with experience in modeling data. Methods or operations of classes of objects are quite different. Here the object-oriented approach becomes more powerful.

The term **method** means something that the object knows how to do—a behavior or responsibility of the object. Many object-oriented developers use this term, but UML also uses the term **operation**. We will use the term "method" in this text, but the terms "method" and "operation" can be used interchangeably.

Doing something implies that a procedure is followed, so methods or operations (whichever term is used) mean procedures. Methods of a class are those procedures the objects in a class know how to follow. With the "object think" approach, these are the things the object knows how to do. These procedures are often defined by using structured programming rules, so object-oriented developers do write procedures.

There are two types of methods—standard methods and custom methods. First, all classes of objects know how to do a few basic things. These are called **standard methods**. Standard methods of a class include knowing how to add a new object, knowing how to show information about an object, knowing how to delete an object, and knowing how to change the values of attributes of an object. These standard methods correspond to database operations such as add, query, delete, and update. Two additional standard methods that are quite common and quite important are knowing how to connect to another object, thereby establishing a relationship, and knowing how to disconnect from another object, thereby breaking a relationship.

A **custom method** is a method that has been custom-designed for a specific class of objects. Custom methods reflect the responsibilities of the objects that the systems analyst needs to identify in the problem domain of the user. The systems analyst should ignore the standard methods that will be added to the classes later during design and implementation and focus his or her attention on the custom methods when initially working with users.

Encapsulation of Attributes and Methods

Encapsulation means that several items are packaged together into one unit. With objects, both the attributes and the methods of the class are packaged together. So, the object knows things (attributes) and knows how to do things (methods). This is what makes the object much more than a data entity. A data entity just has attributes.

Encapsulation allows us to think of the attributes and behaviors of the object as one package. It can help to think of encapsulation as the combining of attributes and methods. On the other hand, encapsulation means something else in the context of object-oriented programming. Encapsulation provides a "cover" or "coating" that hides the internal structure of the object from the environment outside. Other objects (and end users) are prevented from doing anything to the insides of the object. They cannot change the data or change the procedure in a method. Only the methods of the object can change its data, so no unexpected changes can be imposed on the object from the outside. This form of protection is often referred to as **information hiding**. It means we do not have to know how an object works to be able to use it, and it also means we can be confident that an object we are using in a system will not be corrupted.

Messages and Message Sending

Another key concept in the object-oriented approach is **message sending**. When we interact with an object, we send messages to objects, and objects send messages to us (and to each other). Information hiding prevents the end user from changing an object's data; however, the end user can ask the object to invoke, or perform, a method, and the method might change the object's data. Therefore, when we ask an object to do something, we are sending a message to the object, asking it to invoke a method. This is really the same as issuing a command, which is a very familiar concept. Pressing a button, selecting an item from a menu, and dragging and dropping an icon are ways of issuing commands (or sending messages).

An object can also send a message to another object, invoking a method of some type. All of the objects in a class can send the same types of messages, so we usually talk about messages belonging to the class. An object issuing a command to another object is really no different from an end user's command. Again, because the "object think" approach gets us to think of objects as being like us, it becomes easier to visualize a class of objects in a computer system that has this capability.

For example, if the user clicks a cancel button in a dialog box, the button is receiving a message from the user that says, "Go ahead and cancel." The button, in turn, sends a message to the dialog box that says, "Go ahead and close yourself." The dialog box then closes.

On another level, a message might be thought of as an input or an output. When we ask a class of objects to create an object, we must supply the values for the attributes of the object. This is a message much like an input data flow. Similarly, when we ask an object to show us its attribute values or calculate some value for us, the object is producing an output data flow. So, if you think of messages as commands that request services, or as data flowing in and out of the object, the concept should seem familiar.

There is an important link between methods and messages. The message sent to an object must correspond to a method of the object. We can only ask an object to do what it knows how to do, and what it knows how to do are its methods. The complete message includes the object reference (the identity of the object), the method name, and the required data given to the object to be used by the method (the arguments). The method name and list of required arguments are what is needed to interact with the object. This is called the **method signature**.

Polymorphism

A term that is closely related to message sending is **polymorphism**, which literally means multiple forms. Polymorphism is especially relevant for the object-oriented programmer who has to implement messages. Suppose there are three classes of objects—home, boat, and cabin—and we need to calculate property tax for objects in each class. The actual procedure for calculating the tax might be quite different for each class; however, the message "calculate tax" does not need to know which type of class it is being sent to. The same message can always be used, but multiple forms of the calculate tax procedure can be invoked. The ability to send the same message to several different receivers and have the message trigger the right method greatly simplifies the implementation of message sending in object-oriented development.

Consider the message "print" sent to a document, a spreadsheet, an e-mail message, and a Web page. Each of these objects knows how to properly print itself. The sender of the message does not need to know the details, only that the object does indeed know how to respond to the print message. Similarly, a window and a dialog box each know how to properly close when asked. Polymorphism is what allows different objects to respond appropriately to the same command, greatly reducing the complexity of the system.

Inheritance and Generalization/Specialization Hierarchies

Inheritance is the term many people first think of when they think of the object-oriented approach. **Generalization/specialization hierarchies** allow inheritance. As we discussed in Chapter 2, we organize our knowledge on the basis of generalization/specialization hierarchies, we define things in terms of generalization/specialization hierarchies, and we communicate about things in terms of generalization/specialization hierarchies. Learning something new often means we associate a new concept with a previously known concept, and the new concept "inherits" everything known about the previous concept. We add one or more new things, perhaps a new attribute or a new type of behavior, then we make a big deal about the new complex concept we have mastered.

Inherit generally means *get something from*. In the object-oriented approach, one class of objects can inherit attributes and methods from another. Note that it is the ability to remember something (attributes) and the ability to do something (methods) that are inherited—no actual values are involved. The generalization/specialization hierarchy shows a type of relationship, often called an *is a* relationship. One thing *is a* special class of another thing. One thing is everything that the other thing is, but also something more. This is a relationship between classes only. There is no object relationship. For example, a sports car is a special type of car, but it is not related to another specific car.

The generalization/specialization hierarchy and the concept of inheritance are important for several reasons. First, when we ask an end user to describe objects in her problem domain, it can be very natural for the end user to think through what she knows about her work, tracing through the general to the very specific. A specialist has very specialized concepts. As systems analysts, we are interested in obtaining a model of the end user's knowledge, often specialized knowledge, so it makes sense to help the end user to verbalize her knowledge in the same form that she usually organizes her knowledge.

Another important aspect of generalization/specialization hierarchies and inheritance is the way they can streamline the development process. If the analyst knows that the customer class of objects is important to the end user, the analyst may be able to find a general class that is quite similar to the customer class as viewed by the end user. Therefore, the analyst can reuse information about the general class instead of starting from scratch to define the customer class. This is one way that the object-oriented approach encourages and allows *reuse*. Reuse means to use something over again, rather than having to reinvent the wheel. It is also true that generalization/specialization hierarchies allow the analyst to create a more compact and less redundant model, but reuse is the main benefit.

When programming, generalization/specialization hierarchies make it much easier to create a new system, again because of reuse. Some programming languages come with predefined classes of interface objects. The programmer does not have to write all of the code required for including a menu bar on a form in an application; instead, the programmer just adds a predefined menu bar to the form. The form and the menu bar attached to it are finished. With visual programming languages, this takes about a minute.

Object-oriented programming environments usually come with predefined class hierarchies, called class libraries. The object-oriented programmer spends more time searching for classes that are needed and less time defining new classes. Predefined, precoded, and pretested problem domain objects are also increasingly available. If you need to implement a system that includes a rather elaborate generalization/specialization hierarchy for customers of publishing companies, for example, there might be a vendor out there that will sell you one. It might be available in C++, in Java, and in Smalltalk. If you need to make a few changes to it, that is possible, too.

■ Key Terms

aggregation relationships	encapsulation	object reference
association relationships	information hiding	object relationships
attribute	inheritance	operation
cardinality	message sending	polymorphism
class	method	standard methods
composition relationships	method signature	whole-part relationships
custom method	multiplicity	

■ Review Questions

1. Differentiate between a class and an object.

2. What are attributes of a class?

3. What are object relationships?

4. Why is a whole-part relationship a special type of association relationship?

5. What is a method, or operation, of a class?

6. What are the standard methods that any class knows how to provide?

7. What is a custom method?

8. What is encapsulation and what is information hiding?

9. What are messages, and who or what sends them?

10. What is polymorphism?

11. Which type of hierarchy allows inheritance?

12. What two capabilities can a class inherit from another class?

13. How is inheritance related to the potential for reuse?

▌ Discussion Question

1. Discuss the similarities and the differences between data entities and classes of objects. Do you feel the object-oriented approach is "similar" to data modeling, or is it really quite different from data modeling?

▌ Exercises

1. Consider the class named Student at a university:
   a. Describe three "objects" that you know belong to the class.
   b. What are the important attributes of the class?

2. Assuming that the Student class is part of a course registration system at a university, list some of the messages that a registrar might send to it.

3. Assume that the Student class is part of a generalization/specialization hierarchy, with University Person as a general class. What attributes would Student inherit from University Person? What attributes are unique to the Student class, which all University Persons would not have?

4.   A generalization/specialization hierarchy is quite different from a whole-part hierarchy. Consider a hierarchy where a Family contains Family Members. Which type of hierarchy is it? If a system contains this hierarchy and the system includes information only about you, how many objects are there in the system?

5.   Consider a hierarchy where a savings account is a type of account. Which type of hierarchy is it? If a system contains this hierarchy and the system includes information only about your savings account, how many objects are there in the system?

5

Models and UML Notation for the Object-Oriented Approach

- Introduction

- System Development and Models

- Use Cases, Scenarios, and the Use Case Diagram

- The Class Diagram
  Generalization/Specialization Hierarchies
  Object Relationships
  Processing Specifications
  Packages

- Time-Dependent Behavior Models

- Object Interaction Models

- Requirements, System Capability, and Run-Time Behavior

▮ Introduction

In the first four chapters, we emphasized that the object-oriented approach to system development was quite different from traditional approaches, although many system development concepts and techniques from the structured approaches still apply. Chapter 2 explained why the object-oriented approach is a more natural approach for people, because of the way we naturally organize information and learn about the world around us. Chapter 3 described the "object think" approach to viewing objects in information systems to try to get you thinking of objects as knowing things and knowing how to do things. Finally, in Chapter 4, we defined the key terms and concepts that apply to the object-oriented approach.

This chapter focuses specifically on object-oriented system modeling. When you have completed this chapter, you should have a general understanding of the modeling techniques and notation used in this book. The notation is based on UML. To keep things simple, we will not use the full set of notations and facilities found in UML, but will concentrate on the most important aspects.

First, the role of requirements models and design models are discussed. Then we present the most common and important models used with the object-oriented approach. Some of these models are useful for describing the overall capabilities of the system, while others are useful for describing the run-time behavior of the system. Interpreting these models will be emphasized in Chapters 6 and 7, and you will learn about the process of creating some of these models in Chapters 8 and 9.

▮ System Development and Models

The documentation produced during systems analysis and design usually includes a set of *models*. A **model** is a representation of a real thing and emphasizes some aspect of the real thing that is important in a specific context. A model is an *abstraction*, a term we used in Chapter 2. For example, an architect draws a floor plan of a house, which emphasizes the size and placement of the rooms. However, the floor plan does not show how the house will look from the outside. It is an abstraction of the house, showing the aspects of the house that are important when the architect is defining the size and placement of the rooms. On the other hand, the architect might also draw a sketch of how the house will look from the outside, and this model does not show the size and placement of rooms inside. Some graphical models look like the real thing (exterior sketch of the house), but others might not (electrical panel configuration diagram for the house).

Each model emphasizes some aspect of the real-world thing, but many models are required to reveal all of the important details. Further, the models developed must eventually fit together: what is represented in one model (the floor plan) must be consistent with what is represented in another model (the sketch of the exterior of the house). Finally, different models rely on different symbols and notations. Some models are graphical representations, but others are lists or narrative descriptions (such as a list of materials) or even formulas or computations (stiffness required for ceiling joists).

Graphical models, narrative models, and formulas or computational models are all used for object-oriented development. Graphical models are quite useful because they convey a great deal of information in a compact and precise form.

During the systems analysis phase, models are produced to show what information processing is required to be performed by the new system. The set of models produced is often referred to as the requirements model. The requirements model is a logical model, meaning that what is required is shown without indicating how the system might actually be implemented with information technology. The requirements model is therefore technology-independent. Some refer to the requirements model as the essential model, to indicate that the requirements are essential no matter how the system is actually implemented (Yourdon, 1989). A design model, on the other hand, shows how the system will be implemented using technology. Sometimes people also differentiate between a logical and a physical design model. The former will depict a more ideal design, and the latter will describe the design when the actual development environment and programming language are taken into consideration. This indicates that you take on different perspectives as you go along with the modeling process. To be aware of which perspective you are working from is important when you try to decide what details to include and what to defer as you move along in the modeling process.

The requirements model produced during systems analysis does not show how the system will actually be implemented, for several reasons. First, by ignoring technology during systems analysis, the analyst and the users can focus more on the problem to be solved and the essential requirements that must be satisfied by the new system. This reduces the complexity of the analysis process and the requirements models. Second, ignoring technology, makes it is less likely that old ways of doing things will be carried forward into the design of the new system just because limitations in the old technology required things to be done in a certain way in the past.

Finally, by avoiding initial concerns about the way the system might be implemented, the analyst and the users create a model of what is required, while leaving open their options to consider alternative designs later, once the requirements are fully understood. A variety of alternative designs can then be generated based on the same requirements model, and the alternative designs can be evaluated to ensure that the best design is selected for the new system.

Graphical models have been used for quite sometime for requirements models. The structured systems analysis approach involves creating requirements models by using data flow diagrams and an entity-relationship diagram, along with supporting documentation contained in the data dictionary. The data flow diagram and the entity-relationship diagram are graphical models that contain a great deal of information in a form that is easier for people to comprehend than narrative descriptions or more abstract notations.

The data flow diagram is often called a process-oriented model, because it emphasizes the processing that is required by the system. The entity-relationship diagram shows a model of the system's data storage requirements, and it is usually called the data model. Together, these two sets of diagrams support the traditional view of computer systems—that a computer system is a collection of "processes" or computer programs that store data.

Object-oriented analysis (OOA) also involves creating graphical models, but the models emphasize classes of objects and object interactions. The graphical models used and the specific notations are defined by UML. The models and notation presented here are kept simple to facilitate understanding and learning, but the examples cover the main object-oriented constructs in detail.

Use Cases, Scenarios, and the Use Case Diagram

When we analyze a system we try to identify the main functionality that the system will have and the main ways it will be used. If you envision a simple system for a small video rental store, some of the main ways the system would be used include "rent videos" and "add new videos." There would certainly be more. We call each of these ways the system is going to be used a **use case**. More formally a use case is a sequence of actions a system performs that yields an observable result of value to a particular actor. An **actor** is either a person (user) interacting with the system or, in some cases, another system interacting with the system.

A use case captures the main functionality of the system from a user or actor's perspective. It also serves as a vehicle to divide the system into parts that can be implemented somewhat separately. For a given system, we will usually develop and implement the most important use cases first.

Establishing which use cases are important often follows from looking at the main events in the problem domain. For example, a customer rents a video, and the store gets a new video are two events that lead to the use cases "rent videos" and "add new videos." The system must provide the functionality to handle these cases. Each use case requires a sequence of actions from the system. Events are very useful for identifying the use cases that should be documented. Each main event usually corresponds to a use case. Once again, concepts from structured analysis are repackaged and reused in the object-oriented approach, and previous experience with more recent approaches to structured analysis can be successfully applied to the object-oriented approach.

Often you will discover that there are variations in the actions that are required for a use case. When we want to rent videos, the actions required for an existing customer will be somewhat different from those required for a new customer. The sequence of actions required is often referred to as a **scenario**. Each use case has at least one scenario that you can think of as the main scenario. But a use case may also have several more scenarios that you can think of as variations of the main one.

Sometimes it is difficult to decide if a way of using the system should be considered a use case or if it should be considered as a special scenario and thus just a variation or instance of a use case. Do we have one use case "rent videos" or do we have two: "rent videos for existing customer" and "rent videos for new customer." There are no set rules for this. Only experience will help you decide the right granularity. However, early in the analysis process you should try to keep it simple.

Each scenario for the use case will eventually have to be identified and described. One approach for documenting the sequence of actions that constitutes a scenario is to write them out like scripts that highlight how the objects behave when the system operates. Each scenario documents the way the objects (or a small set of the objects) actually behave in a certain situation, and this helps bring the models to life for the analyst and the users.

In Chapter 3 and Chapter 4, we emphasized that the user can be thought of as carrying on a dialog with the objects: the user requests something, and an object responds. In the examples in the chapters that follow, we will document each scenario much like a dialog. The sequence diagram (discussed below) is another way to show the details of a scenario.

By "walking through" each scenario and relating it to the class diagram, it will become apparent which state changes need to take place, which methods will be invoked, and which objects will be interacting. At this stage it becomes evident if the model has the capabilities that are necessary to handle the use case and specific scenario. If it does not, the analyst makes necessary changes to the class diagram.

The use cases we identify are described and documented through a **use case diagram**. The diagram has two main parts. The stick figure symbolizing an actor and the oval indicating the use case. In our video store, the clerk interacts with the two use cases we identified, as shown in Figure 5.1.

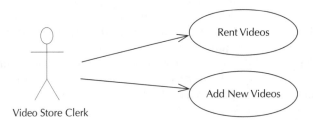

Figure 5.1   Use case diagram example for video store

In addition to the notation depicted in Figure 5.1, use case diagrams can also show relationships between use cases. In UML 1.3 there are three types of relationships—include, generalization, and extend. The **include relationship** (called *uses* in earlier versions of UML) is used when a collection of functionality, organized as a use case, is used in several other use cases. This is very similar to the concept of a subroutine that can be evoked from different places. The relationship is depicted with a dashed arrow directed towards the "subroutine" use case.

The **generalization** and **extend relationships** are very similar. They are used to describe a variation on normal behavior. There are more rules to the extend relationship, and it provides for a more detailed and controlled description than does the generalization relationship. One example of a generalization might be a special use case "rent video to new customer" along with the generalized use case "rent video." Remember the discussion earlier about whether or not to include specialized functionality in the use case diagram. The main rule of thumb we presented is: keep it simple.

The use case diagram serves as a vehicle for a discussion with the user to uncover all needed functionality. It serves much the same purpose as an event-partitioned data flow diagram (DFD) in the traditional structured analysis technique. It provides an overview of the system to use for discussion with users and other analysts. During such discussions, it would become apparent that additional use cases for "return video," "update video information," and "generate rental reports" would be necessary also.

The Class Diagram

The most prominent model produced to capture the static features of the system is called the **class diagram**. It is both a processing requirements model and a data storage requirements model. The class diagram produced during object-oriented analysis is a logical model. It shows what classes of objects are required without showing how the objects might be implemented or how the user might interact with them. The class diagram fits well with the object-oriented view of a computer system—that a computer system is a collection of interacting objects.

What are the classes that are shown on the class diagram? During object-oriented systems analysis, the classes describe the different types of problem domain objects in the work context of the user. Interface objects and operating environment objects are not included. The user interface objects and operating environment objects are added during the design phase because these objects show how the system will be actually implemented with technology.

The symbol for a class of objects is a rectangle, as shown in Figure 5.2. The rectangle is divided into three sections—the name of the class goes in the top section, the attributes of the class go in the middle section, and the methods (or operations) go in the bottom section.

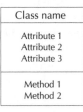

Figure 5.2   A symbol for a class of objects

Generalization/Specialization Hierarchies

Generalization/specialization hierarchies and the concept of inheritance were discussed in Chapter 4. These are core constructs in the object-oriented approach, and the class diagram highlights them. The notation is shown in Figure 5.3. The general class is drawn above the specialized subclasses for readability, and the generalization/specialization hierarchy is indicated by the triangle (closed arrowhead) on the line drawn between classes that points to the general class.

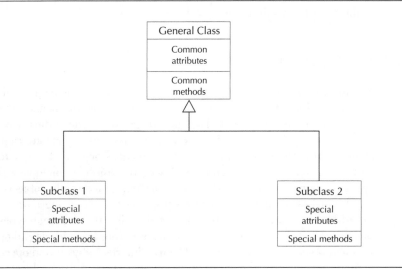

Figure 5.3   Generalization/specialization hierarchy notation

One issue that needs to be addressed when drawing a classification hierarchy is whether or not the subclasses are exhaustive. Exhaustive subclasses cover all possible objects, so the general class will not have any corresponding objects. Such classes are called **abstract classes**. For example, Figure 5.4 shows a general class Person with two subclasses, MalePerson and FemalePerson. Since all people are either male or female, there will never be someone who is just a "person," therefore these two subclasses are exhaustive. The name of the Person class is written in italics to indicate that it is an "empty" or abstract class without objects.

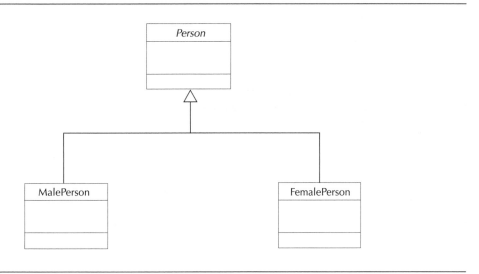

Figure 5.4 Abstract class (in italics) with exhaustive subclass (there are no Person objects)

Object Relationships

The class diagram also includes symbols for relationships among objects. As with relationships in the entity-relationship diagram, an object in one class can be associated with (or connected to) objects in another class. As discussed in Chapter 4, there are two types of object relationships, association (or connection) relationships and whole-part relationships. The whole-part relationship can be viewed as a special (stronger) type of association relationship.

The *association relationship* is quite similar to the relationships typically shown in an entity-relationship diagram. The cardinality or multiplicity of a relationship among objects can be one-to-one, one-to-many, or many-to-many. Figure 5.5 shows an example of two classes of objects, where each object in the class on the left is associated with many objects in the class on the right. The numbers and symbols representing cardinality/multiplicity include a "1" for one and an asterisk (*) for many.

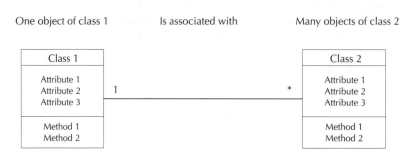

Figure 5.5   Two classes with an association relationship (multiplicity is shown as 1 and * on association line)

Additional numbers and symbols are often added to indicate optional or mandatory relationships. Often these are referred to as minimum and maximum cardinality/multiplicity. In the example shown in Figure 5.6, the symbols on the right side of the relationship tell us that a given object of Class 1 can be related to *zero* (minimum) but possibly *many* (maximum) Class 2 objects. Read in the other direction, a given Class 2 object is related to *at least one* Class 1 object and also *at most one* Class 1 object. In other words, it is always related to one and only one Class 1 object and is thus a mandatory relationship.

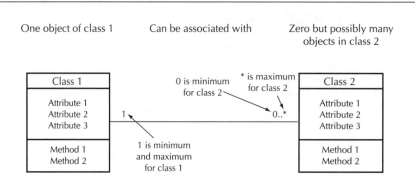

Figure 5.6   Minimum and maximum cardinality (multiplicity)

The *whole-part relationship* is usually called an aggregation relationship. This relationship is basically depicted the same way as an association relationship, with the same use of minimum and maximum cardinality/multiplicity. A diamond at the whole end of the association is added to the line representing the relationship to set it apart from the association relationships in the model. For readability we generally try to draw this relationship vertically with the whole above the parts, as shown in Figure 5.7.

UML distinguishes between ordinary aggregation relationships, depicted by an open diamond, and composition (depicted by a filled in diamond). Ordinary aggregations can be entirely conceptual and basically just highlight what is the whole and what is the part in the association. Composition is a stronger relationship—the part cannot exist without the whole.

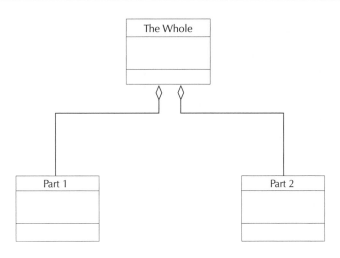

Figure 5.7   Whole-part relationships (aggregation)

Processing Specifications

In the class diagram, methods are usually referred to by a verb and a noun, for example "calculate fee." The procedure to be followed when performing the method will usually have to be described in detail. This can be done using any of the process-modeling techniques that are known from traditional system development. Pseudocode, structured English, action diagrams, and program flowcharts are some of the alternatives that are available. The methods called for in business-oriented information systems usually are quite simple, and some form of pseudocode or structured English is usually adequate. No matter which approach is used, the method name in the class diagram indicates that the process followed is described elsewhere.

Packages

If the class diagram becomes large, it will be quite difficult to use for an overview of the system. In such cases it might be necessary to create a high-level view of the system, using some kind of partitioning or clustering scheme. Clustering can be done after the initial model is produced to facilitate presentation and further work, or beforehand to allow for division of work between workgroups from the outset. UML calls these clusters **packages** and provides a modeling notation called a package diagram.

Time-Dependent Behavior Models

The class diagram captures much of the important system capabilities. Another graphical model, called the **statechart**, is often used to document more complex behavior of an object. A state chart shows the states an object might be in and the actions or conditions that cause an object to make a transition from one state to another.

It is important to understand both the possible states of an object and the allowed sequence that changes in states must follow. For example, a potential student might apply to the university, be accepted as a regular student, and then eventually graduate. The three possible states are potential student, enrolled student, and graduated student. A potential student cannot be changed to a graduated student without first being an enrolled student. Therefore, the statechart models some of the rules that apply in the work context of the user and shows the behavior (state transitions) the objects exhibit. Since the transitions are related to the passing of time, the term **time-dependent behavior** is often used to describe what is being modeled.

Statecharts can be viewed as extensions of the class diagram, and you could conceivably create one statechart for every class in your class diagram. However, in practice, you will only create a statechart for those classes that exhibit especially interesting or complex time-dependent behavior. A simple example using the UML notation is shown in Figure 5.8. The states are depicted by boxes. The transitions are shown as arrows between boxes, showing that an object in one state can change to another state. There is a start state and an end state depicted by the solid dots.

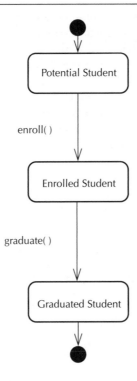

Figure 5.8   Statechart showing state transitions for the Student class

Statecharts or state transition diagrams are also used for modeling real-time system requirements and user-computer interaction dialogs in traditional system development. There are many variations of the state transition diagram, and there are other diagrams that are also used to model time-dependent behavior (such as the entity life history diagram). Additionally, there is nothing inherently object-oriented about the state transition diagram.

Object Interaction Models

The use case and its scenarios serve as a vehicle for organizing the object interactions that take place. Each scenario involves a certain set of interactions. If the interactions related to a scenario are complex, it might be difficult to keep track of them. Some kind of modeling technique is required to convey complex interaction patterns; otherwise, the interactions that are involved might not be evident from the description of the scenario.

UML uses two different notations and models for object interaction diagrams—one is called a **sequence diagram**, and the other a **collaboration diagram**. The sequence diagram presents object interaction arranged in time sequence. It shows the objects involved in the scenario and the sequence of messages that are exchanged. The collaboration diagram shows interaction organized around the objects and their messages to each other. The two are more or less interchangeable, and some CASE tools will automatically generate one from the other. Which one to use is largely a matter of taste, although the sequence diagram seems to be the one most people prefer. For simplicity, we limit the examples to sequence diagrams, as shown in Figure 5.9.

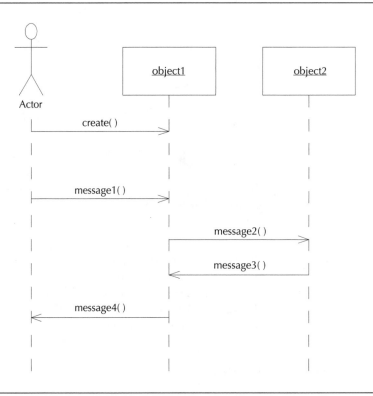

Figure 5.9   Sequence diagram notation (Actor, Objects, Lifelines, and Messages)

Sequence diagrams show interactions among objects and with outside actors for a specific scenario or instance of a use case. Each object is represented as a rectangle with the class name underlined to indicate that it is an object or instance of the class. The actor is a stick figure, as in the use case diagram. The vertical line below the actor and each object is called the **lifeline** of the object. UML can differentiate between active and passive objects by different forms of the lifeline.

Messages are shown as horizontal arrows from an actor to an object, from an object to another object, or from an object to an actor. Messages therefore represent the interaction. The sequence in which the messages are sent is indicated from top to bottom. The diagram is read from the top down, so the uppermost message is the first and the lower the last. Messages go to the lifeline unless a new instance of a class needs to be created, in which case the message to create a new instance goes to the rectangle representing the object, as shown in create() message in Figure 5.9.

Requirements, System Capability, and Run-Time Behavior

The use case diagram provides a view of the needed functionality of the system, from a user perspective. The class diagram shows what the system can remember and what it can do, providing a picture of the capability of the total system. The sequence diagram provides a view of how one particular scenario is played out. There will usually be one use case diagram, one class diagram, and then a number of sequence diagrams. As you go through the modeling process more details are added to the different models and they are harmonized, so they are all consistent with each other. Together they create an extensive and integrated picture of the system to be built.

Key Terms

abstract classes	include relationship	statechart
actor	lifeline	time-dependent behavior
class diagram	model	use case
collaboration diagram	packages	use case diagram
extend relationship	scenario	
generalization relationship	sequence diagram	

Review Questions

1. What is a model, and why are graphical models useful for system development?

2. What is the difference between a requirements model and a design model?

3. What are the reasons for creating logical models?

4. What is the difference between an event and use case?

5. What is the difference between a use case and a scenario?

6. What are the UML graphical models used in the object-oriented approach?

7. What items are listed in the three sections of the symbol for a class?

8. What symbol is used to indicate a generalization/specialization?

9. How is an association relationship shown on a class diagram?

10. What symbol is used to indicate a whole-part/aggregation relationship?

11. How are minimum and maximum cardinality/multiplicity indicated?

12. What are the symbols for a state and a state transition in a statechart?

13. How might the processing details of a method be documented?

14. In the object-oriented approach, which model is used to document interactions in a scenario?

▌ Discussion Question

1. Discuss the extent to which the models used with the object-oriented approach are similar to the models used with the traditional structured approach.

▌ Exercises

1. Draw a class diagram showing one class: Student. Include the attributes you listed in the exercise in Chapter 4. Expand the class diagram by drawing a generalization/specialization hierarchy with Student as a sub-class of University Person, including attributes you listed in the exercise in Chapter 4.

2. Draw a class diagram with two classes, Student and Major. Add some attributes for Major, and assume that a Student can enroll in many Majors, and that a Major can enroll many Students. Further, assume that a Major can enroll a minimum of zero and a maximum of many Students, but a Student must enroll in at least one, but possibly many, Majors.

3. Draw a class diagram with a whole-part (aggregation) relationship for Family and Family Members, described in the exercises in Chapter 4. Assume that a Family Member must be part of one but possibly many Families, and that a Family might contain zero of possibly many Family Members.

4. Draw a statechart showing the two states of a lamp: turned on and turned off.

5. Draw a sequence diagram showing the following scenario:

   Actor asks TV to turn on.

   TV asks Lamp to lower light level.

   TV asks Actor which channel to set itself to.

   Actor tells TV to set channel to channel 13.

References

Booch, G., Rumbaugh, J. and Jacobson, I. *The Unified Modeling Language Reference Manual*. Reading, Massachusetts: Addison-Wesley, 1999.

Booch, G., Rumbaugh, J. and Jacobson, I. *The Unified Modeling Language Users Guide*. Reading, Massachusetts: Addison-Wesley, 1999.

Fowler, M. *UML Distilled (2nd ed.)*. Reading, Massachusetts: Addison-Wesley, 2000.

Jacobson, I. et al. *Object Oriented Software Engineering: A Use Case Driven Approach*. Reading, Massachusetts: Addison-Wesley, 1992.

Kulak, D., Guiney, E. and Lavkulik, E. *Use Cases: Requirements in Context*. Reading, Massachusetts: Addison-Wesley (ACM Press), 2000.

Yourdon, E. *Modern Structured Analysis*. Englewood Cliffs, New Jersey: Prentice Hall, 1989.

6

Understanding Simple Object-Oriented Requirements Models

Introduction

The object-oriented approach involves creating models that define the requirements, the design, and then the implementation of a computer system. This chapter emphasizes how to read and interpret some of the requirements models, using the "object think" approach to bring the objects to life. When you have completed this chapter, you should understand how to interpret the behavior of objects in a system, through the use of use cases, class diagrams, sequence diagrams, and written scenarios.

A System with a Single Class of Objects

The best way to begin to understand an object-oriented system is to start with a very simple example. Suppose you collect video tapes for your personal viewing pleasure. You require a computer system that will store information about your videos. The problem domain object of importance might be named a VideoItem, so the requirements for your system include a class named VideoItem. The class diagram for your system is shown in Figure 6.1.

Figure 6.1   A class diagram with one class

What do we know about your requirements just by looking at this class diagram? First, we know that the class allows us to store information about any number of videos. Based on the listed attributes, we can store the title and date you acquired the video. No custom methods are indicated, so the class is limited to standard methods.

Let's try the "object think" approach to try to understand the capabilities of this system. The class named VideoItem knows things, and it knows how to do things:

I am a VideoItem.

I know my Title and my Date Acquired.

I know how to show my attribute values.

I know how to create myself.

I know how to delete myself.

I know how to change the values of my attributes.

I know how to associate myself with other objects, but I don't see any other classes of objects around here to connect to.

Since you want to be able to add new videos, see information about your videos, possibly change or correct the information, and delete videos, these are potential uses for the system that define the requirements—four use cases. The use case diagram for the system is shown in Figure 6.2. The VideoItem class has standard methods that provide the required capabilities. It seems to satisfy all of the requirements that you have for your simple system.

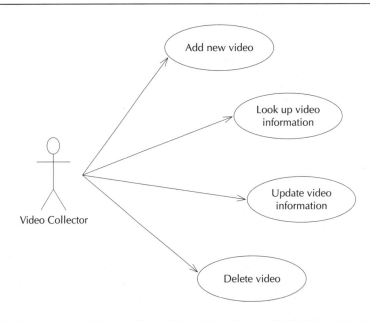

Figure 6.2   Use Case diagram for Video Collector

The power of the object-oriented approach begins to become apparent when you consider how much information the analyst *avoids* having to specify for your system. No procedures have to be written. All of the required processing is included in the standard methods that all classes know about. A separate data model is not required. All of the data storage requirements are included because the class has attributes that define the pieces of data that must be stored.

Data flow definitions are not really needed either, even though we know there are input and output requirements. Obviously, when a new video is added the user will have to supply the Title and the Date Acquired. Obviously, when a video is deleted the user will have to identify the video to be deleted.

To verify that all requirements are satisfied, it is important to walk through all of the desired use cases required by the user. The use cases are identified by looking for events that might cause the user to interact with the system. Recall that each use case might have more than one scenario. Each scenario might be documented as follows:

1. **Event: You get a new video.**
   Use Case: Add new video, main scenario

   The user sends a message to VideoItem asking it to add a new VideoItem object.

   VideoItem knows that it needs the Title and the Date Acquired to add a new VideoItem, so it asks the user for those values.

   The user supplies the Title and the Date Acquired.

   The VideoItem class adds the new VideoItem and tells the user the task is complete.

2. **Event: You want to see a list of all of your videos.**
   Use Case: Look up video information, main scenario

   The user sends a message to VideoItem asking it to show the attribute values of all of its objects.

   VideoItem lists the attribute values of all the videos.

3. **Event: You want to correct some information about a video.**
   Use Case: Update video information, main scenario

   The user sends a message to VideoItem asking it to change some information about a video.

   VideoItem knows that it needs the Title of the video to correct, so it asks the user for the Title.

   The user supplies the Title.

   VideoItem asks the user for the corrected Title and/or the corrected Date Acquired.

   The user supplies the corrected Title and/or corrected Date Acquired to VideoItem.

   VideoItem changes the value(s) and tells the user the task is complete.

4. **Event: You lose or damage one of your videos.**
   Use Case: Delete video, main scenario

   The user sends a message to VideoItem asking it to delete a VideoItem.

   VideoItem knows that it needs the Title of the video to delete, so it asks the user for the Title.

   The user supplies the Title.

   VideoItem deletes the object with that Title and tells the user the task is complete.

Each scenario can also be modeled using a sequence diagram. The sequence diagram shows the object interactions described above in a graphical view. One example is shown in Figure 6.3, for the use case "Add new video."

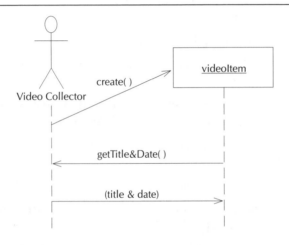

Figure 6.3   Sequence diagram for Add New Video scenario

A Single Class with a Custom Method

To illustrate when it might be necessary to define a custom method for a class diagram, the VideoItem example can be changed to reflect different requirements. Suppose you want to store some additional information about your videos: the number of times you have viewed a video and the date you last viewed the video.

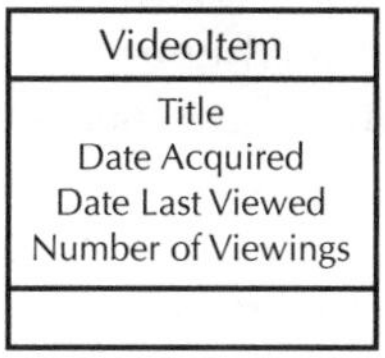

```
                    ┌─────────────────────┐
                    │      VideoItem       │
                    ├─────────────────────┤
                    │        Title         │
                    │    Date Acquired     │
                    │   Date Last Viewed   │
                    │  Number of Viewings  │
                    │                      │
                    └─────────────────────┘
```

Figure 6.4   A single class with additional attributes

Two additional attributes are added: Date Last Viewed and Number of Viewings. The class diagram with these additional attributes is shown in Figure 6.4. Using the "object think" approach:

I am a VideoItem.

> I know my Title, Date Acquired, Date Last Viewed, and Number of Viewings.
>
> I know how to show my attribute values.
>
> I know how to create myself.
>
> I know how to delete myself.
>
> I know how to change the values of my attributes.
>
> I know how to connect to other objects, but I don't see any other classes of objects around here to connect to.

These capabilities satisfy most of your requirements, but you also want to tell VideoItem to record a viewing of the video. "Record viewing" is an additional use case that would be added to the use case diagram. Again using "object think," this time to clarify what a class does not know how to do:

I am a VideoItem.

> Someone told me to record a viewing of a VideoItem, but I don't know how to do that!

Since VideoItem does not know what to do, you could ask VideoItem to show the attribute values of the video, write down the number of viewings, and then ask VideoItem to change the value of Date Last Viewed to the date you viewed the video. You could then add one to the number of viewings and ask VideoItem to change that attribute value, too. However, shouldn't the computer system handle the details of this processing for you?

Therefore, we need to define a custom method for VideoItem so it will know what processing to do anytime it is sent a message that a video has been viewed.

A reasonable name for this service is Record Viewing, which has been added to the class diagram shown in Figure 6.5. The specification, which the analyst would be required to write, might look something like this:

Record Viewing method:

    set Date Last Viewed = viewing date

    set Number of Viewings = Number of Viewings + 1

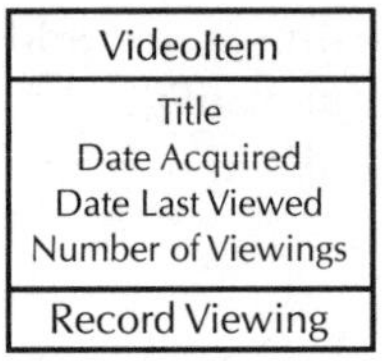

```
┌─────────────────────────┐
│       VideoItem         │
├─────────────────────────┤
│          Title          │
│      Date Acquired      │
│     Date Last Viewed    │
│    Number of Viewings   │
├─────────────────────────┤
│     Record Viewing      │
└─────────────────────────┘
```

Figure 6.5   A single class with a custom method

To verify that all requirements are now satisfied, the use cases can be expanded to include the case where the user has viewed a video, written in the form of a scenario as shown in Event 5:

5. **Event: You view a video.**
   Use Case: Record viewing, main scenario

   The user sends a message to VideoItem asking it to record the viewing of a video.

   VideoItem knows it needs the Title and the date viewed, so it asks the user for these values.

   The user supplies the Title and date viewed.

   VideoItem locates the object with that Title, changes Date Last Viewed to date viewed, adds one to the Number of Viewings (by following the instructions in its Method named Record Viewing), and tells the user the task is complete.

The sequence diagram that models the object interactions for this scenario is shown in Figure 6.6.

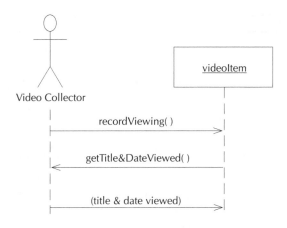

Figure 6.6   Sequence diagram for Record Viewing scenario

Two Classes with a Message

The system with one class described above emphasizes how the class diagram, along with the use cases and scenarios, documents system requirements, both data storage requirements and processing requirements. Both standard methods and a custom method were demonstrated. The example also shows how important it is to begin using both the "object think" approach and scenarios to work through the capabilities of the system.

But information systems usually include more than one class, and the objects in these classes usually interact. Therefore, we will extend the VideoItem example to include an additional class, where there is a relationship between the objects.

Suppose your video collection expands, and you now own many copies of each video. We can now identify two classes in your problem domain. First, you collect Videos, which have a Title and Type (comedy, drama, adventure, etc.). But you actually view a VideoItem that represents one of the videos. Each VideoItem has attributes for Item Number, Format, Date Last Viewed, and Number of Viewings. You might have many of these VideoItems for each Video title. Therefore, we need a one-to-many association relationship between Video and VideoItem.

Figure 6.7   Class diagram with two classes and an association relationship

You do not plan to store information about a video unless you have a corresponding VideoItem in your collection, so the relationship is mandatory. Each Video object must be associated with one or more VideoItem objects, and each VideoItem object must be associated with exactly one Video. Figure 6.7 shows an initial class diagram (which includes the notation for minimum and maximum cardinality/multiplicity, indicating that the relationship is mandatory). You still want to record the viewing of each VideoItem. Use the "object think" approach for each class:

I am a Video.

> I know my Title and Type (comedy, drama, etc.).
>
> I know what VideoItems I am associated with.
>
> I know how to show my attribute values.
>
> I know how to create myself.
>
> I know how to delete myself.
>
> I know how to change the values of my attributes.
>
> I know how to associate myself with VideoItem objects.

I am a VideoItem.

> I know my Item Number, Format, Date Last Viewed, and Number of Viewings.
>
> I know what Video I am associated with, and I must be associated with exactly one Video.
>
> I know how to show my attribute values.
>
> I know how to create myself.
>
> I know how to delete myself.

I know how to change the values of my attributes.

I know how to associate myself with a Video object.

I know how to record a viewing.

Again, we have quite a few capabilities reflected in the class diagram. As the user of the system, you think in terms of VideoItems. You never plan to add a Video if you do not have a corresponding VideoItem. You do not lose or damage a Video, you lose or damage a VideoItem. The same logic might hold for having Record Viewing as a method of VideoItem. You view a VideoItem not a Video. But as always, you need to look to the work context of the user and then adjust the model to reflect the requirements. If the user wants to know the last viewing date of each individual VideoItem, we will let VideoItem be responsible for recording viewing. If what she really wanted was to know the last time she viewed this video, without caring about which copy, we should let the Video object be responsible for recording the viewing. This is a good example of how the placement of responsibilities in the class diagram leads to different capabilities. It is important that you are able to understand the implications of the class diagram, so that you can make sure the capabilities match what the user wants.

From the user's point of view, the scenario followed when the user gets a new copy of a video is as follows:

1. **Event: You get a new video.**
   Use Case: Add new video item, main scenario

   The user sends a message to VideoItem asking it to add a new VideoItem object.

   VideoItem knows that it needs the Format to add a new VideoItem, so it asks the user for that value.

   The user supplies the Format.

   VideoItem also knows it must connect to the correct Video object, so it asks the user for the Title of the Video that it should connect to.

   The user supplies the Title.

   VideoItem adds the new VideoItem object, assigns an item number, connects to the Video object with the supplied Title, and tells the user the task is complete.

The sequence diagram that corresponds to the scenario above is shown in Figure 6-8. Note that a VideoItem object interacts directly with a Video object by sending a message. In a very real way, the system is a collection of interacting objects.

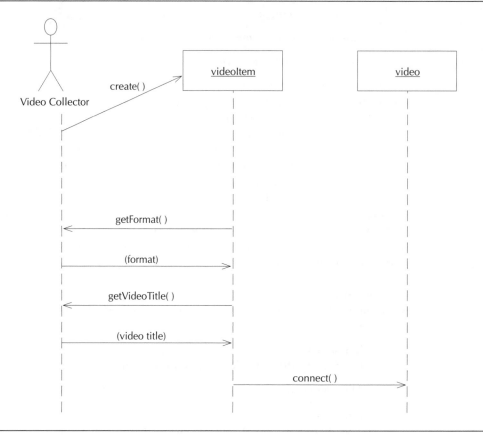

Figure 6.8   Sequence diagram for Add New Video scenario

However, suppose the video is the first copy of the video that you have obtained. This is an example where there can be more than one scenario for a use case. Isn't this the more common case? Using the "object think" approach:

I am a VideoItem.

Someone asked me to add a new VideoItem object, but I can't find a Video with that Title to connect to! I don't know what to do!

The user could solve this problem by first asking Video to add a Video object for the new video, supplying the Title and the Type. Then the user could ask VideoItem to add the new VideoItem, and the VideoItem object would be able to connect to the correct Video object. But shouldn't the computer system handle this common case more directly? Is it reasonable to ask the user to add a Video first when the user thinks in terms of VideoItems?

Therefore, we need to add to the capabilities of the VideoItem class to better fit the user's requirements. We can solve the problem by defining a message that VideoItem sends to Video requesting that Video add a new Video object whenever VideoItem cannot find a Video to connect to. Using the "object think" approach:

I am a VideoItem.

I know how to add a new VideoItem object and connect to the correct Video object.

If the correct Video object does not exist, I know how to ask Video to add a new Video object, and when it is done doing so, I will connect to it.

I am a Video.

I know how to add a new Video object, and I can do so whenever I receive the request, either from the user or from another object.

The scenario for adding a new VideoItem would be the same as shown previously for the case where the new VideoItem is the second copy in your collection. However, when it is the first copy, the scenario is different:

1B. Event: You get a new video.
Use case: Add new video item
Scenario: Add new video item when it is the first copy

The user sends a message to VideoItem asking it to add a new VideoItem object.

VideoItem knows that it needs the Format to add a new VideoItem, so it asks the user for that value.

The user supplies the Format.

VideoItem also knows it must connect to the correct Video object, so it asks the user for the Title of the Video that it should connect to.

The user supplies the Title.

VideoItem attempts to connect to the correct Video, but cannot find it. Therefore, VideoItem sends a message to Video asking it to add a Video object with the Title.

Video knows it must have the Type (comedy, drama, etc.) to add a Video object, so it asks the user for the Type.

The user supplies the Type to Video.

Video adds the Video object, using the Title supplied by VideoItem and the Type supplied by the user, and tells VideoItem the task is complete.

VideoItem adds the new VideoItem object, assigns an item number, connects to the correct Video object, and tells the user the task is complete.

The sequence diagram that corresponds to the scenario above is shown in Figure 6.9. Note that the new VideoItem object creates the new Video object, which in turn interacts with the user to get the needed information about itself.

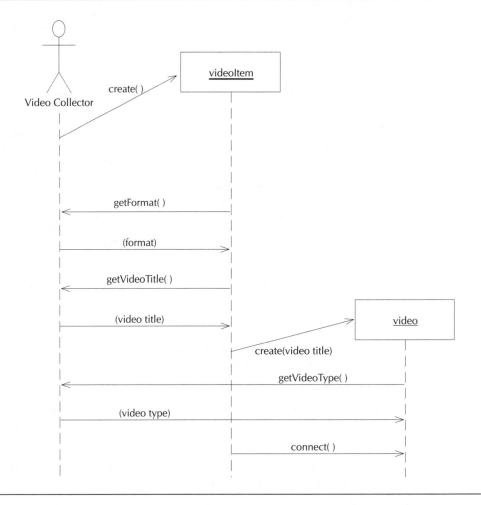

Figure 6.9   Sequence diagram for Add New Video Item when it is the First Copy scenario

Comparison of the Class Diagram with a Data Flow Diagram

The structured analysis approach uses the data flow diagram to create a logical model of the system. The more recent approaches to structured analysis also decompose the system into subprocesses based on events. The scenarios used for the system with two classes above also used events to document the behavior of the system, in this case there were five events, resulting in five use cases.

How would the data flow diagram for the same system look? The data flow diagram is similar to the use case diagram in that it shows the external agent as the source and destination of data and decomposes into processes based on events. The DFD contains more details, though. Figure 6.10 shows a data flow diagram that provides a model of the system at the diagram 0 level, also called the event-partitioned system model. Since there are five events, there are five processes shown. These five processes all receive inputs from and provide outputs to one external agent, the Video Collector. There are two data stores, corresponding to an entity-relationship diagram with two data entities connected by a one-to-many relationship.

The complete structured analysis documentation would include a context diagram, diagram 0 (shown), the entity-relationship model, process descriptions for the five processes, data flow definitions, and data element definitions. The class diagram in Figure 6.7 implies exactly the same capabilities, but the model is much more concise and compact, and this greatly reduces the complexity of the model. The use case diagram, the scenarios, and the sequence diagrams verify and complete the details of the system requirements.

This example is quite simple, but with more complex systems, the difference in model complexity can be very important. And, just as we can assume the objects know how to do the standard methods, we can begin to make assumptions about standard scenarios. Many of them can be left undocumented. Or, better yet, we can reuse them!

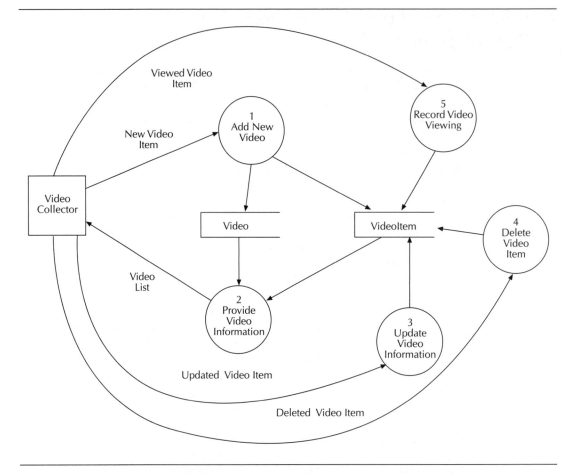

Figure 6.10   Data flow diagram showing comparable Video Collector requirements

Review Questions

1. What does the class of objects VideoItem, in Figure 6.1, know and know how to do?

2. What class is responsible for interacting with the user in all four use cases shown in the use case diagram in Figure 6.2?

3. Explain why the custom method Record Viewing is needed if we want the system to handle more of the processing instead of assuming the user will do it?

4. What is the minimum and maximum cardinality/multiplicity of the relationship between Video and VideoItem in Figure 6.7.

5. What does the message from VideoItem to Video in Figure 6.8 say to the Video?

6. List the pieces of documentation that the structured approach would produce to define the same requirements that the object-oriented approach defines.

Discussion Question

1. The data flow diagram in Figure 6.10 documents the requirements for a system that is very much the same as the system documented by the UML models. Discuss whether the actual system developed will either be object-oriented or not, depending upon the type of *requirements model* developed by the analyst.

Exercises

1. Convert the two-class model shown in Figure 6.7 to a model of a system used by a library with books and many copies of each book. Write a scenario description for the event "the library gets its first copy of a book." Draw a sequence diagram that matches the scenario.

2. Consider the following change to the user's requirements for the class diagram shown in Figure 6.7. The video collector decides to only record the viewing of a Video and does not care which VideoItem was actually viewed. Change the class diagram accordingly, and rewrite the main scenario in response to the event "Collector views a videotape."

3. Assume that the user in the exercise above wants to be able to find out both the last viewing of each individual VideoItem and the last viewing of the Video object. What changes would you make to the model?

4. Assume that the video collector begins loaning videotapes to friends and relatives. Naturally, it is important to know who has each videotape at any point in time. Additionally, it is important to know when each video was borrowed and returned. Expand the object model to allow for these requirements.

7

Understanding More Complex Requirements Models with Generalization/Specialization and Whole-Part Hierarchies

Introduction

One important aspect of the object-oriented approach is the process of organizing the information system into a set of generalization/specialization hierarchies and whole-part hierarchies. A generalization/specialization hierarchy allows one class to inherit attributes and methods from another. A whole-part hierarchy shows object relationships between an object in one class and objects in other classes that make up its "parts."

This chapter emphasizes these aspects of object-oriented requirements models, by again giving relatively simple examples. When you have completed this chapter, you should understand how to interpret generalization/specialization hierarchies and use inheritance. Additionally, you should understand whole-part hierarchies and some of the benefits of using them in object-oriented requirements models.

A System with a Generalization/Specialization Hierarchy

The generalization/specialization hierarchy shows a hierarchy of classes and subclasses that lead from the general to the specific. As discussed in Chapter 4, generalization/specialization hierarchies can help the analyst reuse existing classes and make the model less redundant and more compact.

Suppose you work for a medical clinic that needs to store some basic information about doctors and patients. The classes of objects in the problem domain obviously include doctors and patients. You want to store information about each doctor, such as name, date of birth, date employed, and specialty. Similarly, you want to store information about each patient, such as name, date of birth, employer, and insurance company.

These two classes have something in common. Both have names and dates of birth as attributes. In fact, all people have names and dates of birth, so we can use a general class called Person. Some people are doctors and some people are patients. For doctors, we want to know their date of employment and their specialty. For patients, on the other hand, we want to know their employer and insurance company. Therefore, we need to define specialized classes for these two types of people because each has different attributes.

Figure 7.1 shows the class diagram for this system. The two classes are DoctorPerson and PatientPerson. Person is also shown, as a general class. The generalization/specialization hierarchy is indicated by the triangle symbol on the line that connects Person to DoctorPerson and PatientPerson.

This system does not require that we store information about a person unless they are either a doctor or a patient, therefore Person is an abstract class that exists only to allow subclasses to inherit from it.

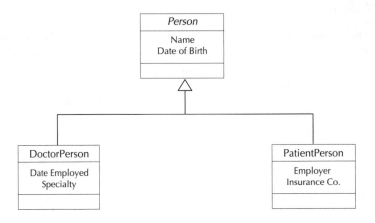

Figure 7.1   Generalization/specialization hierarchy for the medical clinic showing inheritance (Person is an abstract class)

When we store information about a doctor, DoctorPerson will include values for Name and Date of Birth. Similarly, when we store information about a patient, PatientPerson will include values for Name and Date of Birth. Therefore, both DoctorPerson and PatientPerson "inherit" the attributes Name and Date of Birth from the general class named Person. However, it is important to recognize that neither inherits specific values, unless there are default values.

To explore the capabilities of this system, use the "object think" approach:

I am a PatientPerson.

I am a special type of Person.

I know my Employer and Insurance Company.

Since I am a special type of Person, I know my Name and Date of Birth.

I know how to create myself. And when I do, I require values for Employer and Insurance Company plus values for Name and Date of Birth, attributes I inherit from my general class.

I am a DoctorPerson.

I am a special type of Person.

I know my Date Employed and my Specialty.

Since I am a special type of Person, I know my Name and Date of Birth.

I know how to create myself. And when I do, I require values for Date Employed and Specialty plus values for Name and Date of Birth, attributes I inherit from my general class.

The "object think" approach would also indicate the capability to show information about a DoctorPerson or a PatientPerson and to change information about them. The requirements for the system could be described by scenarios that highlight the user's interaction with the system, organized around events that occur and their corresponding use cases.

1. **Event: A doctor is employed with the clinic.**
   Use Case: Add new doctor, main scenario

   The user sends a message to DoctorPerson asking it to add a new DoctorPerson object.

   DoctorPerson knows it needs the Name, Date of Birth, Date Employed, and Specialty to add a DoctorPerson object, so it asks the user for those values.

   The user supplies the requested values.

   DoctorPerson adds the new DoctorPerson object and tells the user the task is complete.

2. **Event: A new patient is added to the clinic.**
   Use Case: Add new patient, main scenario

   The user sends a message to PatientPerson asking it to add a new PatientPerson object.

   PatientPerson knows it needs the Name, Date of Birth, Insurance Company, and Employer to add a PatientPerson object, so it asks the user for those values.

   The user supplies the requested values.

   PatientPerson adds the new PatientPerson object and tells the user the task is complete.

Again, notice that the user has no reason to add a Person, unless the person is either a DoctorPerson or a PatientPerson. Therefore, there are no objects in this system for the class Person. Also, use cases and scenarios related to other events should be included to clarify the requirements. Obviously the user wants to look up information about doctors and patients. This query capability is implicit. For example, the user could ask to see all of the doctors with a specific specialty. Similarly, the user could ask to see all patients with a specific insurance company. If specific query requirements are important for the user, these can be documented. Otherwise, we can assume these capabilities exist. No custom methods are required to meet the requirements.

Sequence diagrams modeling the interactions in the scenarios described above are shown in Figures 7.2 and 7.3.

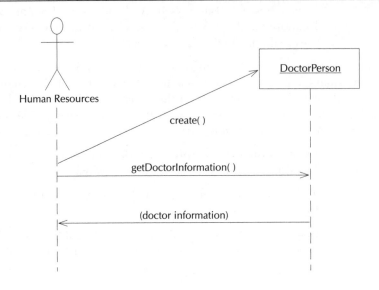

Figure 7.2   Sequence diagram for Add New Doctor scenario

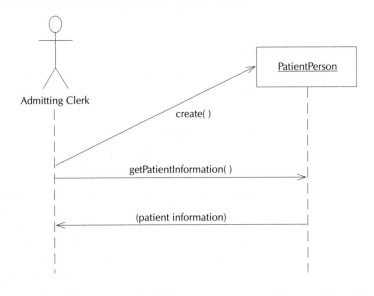

Figure 7.3   Sequence diagram for Add New Patient scenario

A Generalization/Specialization Hierarchy Associated with Another Class

Generalization/specialization hierarchies, such as the DoctorPerson and PatientPerson example on the previous page, are usually only part of the problem domain of a system. The clinic is mainly concerned with providing treatments to patients, so information about treatments should also be included in the system. Therefore, we will expand this example to provide for this requirement. The expanded class diagram is shown in Figure 7.4.

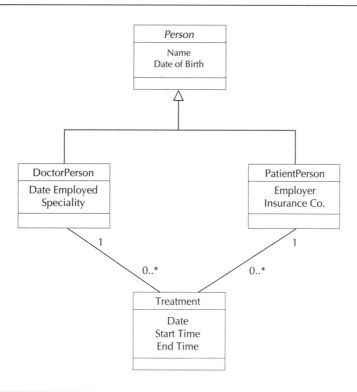

Figure 7.4   Treatment class associated with DoctorPerson and PatientPerson for the medical clinic

The problem domain and corresponding class diagram now include one more class, called Treatment. The attributes of Treatment (required by this system) are the Date, Start Time, and End Time. Each Treatment is associated with one

PatientPerson. Each Treatment is also associated with one DoctorPerson. Therefore, we know who was treated and who provided the treatment. Naturally, a DoctorPerson provides many Treatments. Similarly, a PatientPerson might receive many Treatments. These associations are shown on the class diagram, using cardinality/multiplicity notation written on the association relationship line. The Treatment class is quite similar to an associative (or intersection) data entity type in the entity-relationship diagram. But because Treatment is a class, it knows things and it knows how to do things. Using the "object think" approach:

I am a Treatment.

I know my Date, Start Time, and End Time.

I know what DoctorPerson I am associated with, and I must be associated with exactly one.

I know what PatientPerson I am associated with, and I must be associated with exactly one.

I know how to create myself.

I know how to associate myself with a DoctorPerson.

I know how to associate myself with a PatientPerson.

I am a DoctorPerson.

I know which Treatments I am associated with, if any.

I am a PatientPerson.

I know which Treatments I am associated with, if any.

DoctorPerson and PatientPerson also know how to associate themselves with a Treatment, but the relationship is optional. An optional relationship means that a doctor might not have treated any patients, or a patient might not have received a treatment. These classes of objects also have all of the capabilities listed previously. The requirements can be clarified by thinking through some scenarios.

1. **Event: A doctor is employed with the clinic.**
   Use Case: Add new doctor, main scenario

   The interaction is the same as shown previously. Note that there is no requirement that the DoctorPerson object connect to a Treatment, even though this capability is present.

2. **Event: A new patient is added to the clinic.**
   Use Case: Add new patient, main scenario

   The interaction is the same as shown previously. Note that there is no requirement that the PatientPerson object connect to a Treatment, even though this capability is present.

3. **Event: A patient receives a treatment.**
   Use Case: Record a treatment, main scenario

   The user sends a message to Treatment asking it to add a new Treatment object.

   Treatment knows it needs to know the DoctorPerson Name and the PatientPerson Name because it is required to connect to both objects, so it asks the user for these values.

   The user supplies these values.

   Treatment knows it needs the Date, Start Time, and End Time for the Treatment object, so it asks the user for these values.

   The user supplies these values.

   The Treatment class adds a new Treatment object, using the Date, Start Time, and End Time, connects to the correct DoctorPerson object, connects to the correct PatientPerson object, and tells the user the task is complete.

The scenarios can clarify the requirements for the system, which might be more restricted than the capabilities implied by the object model. For example, a DoctorPerson object will not be required to connect to Treatment objects. The user will add a DoctorPerson before any treatments are given. Similarly, the user will add a PatientPerson before treatments are given. These sequences follow from the user's work domain. Doctors are employed, and information is added about doctors as part of the employment process before they can treat patients. Similarly, new patients are screened for insurance prior to receiving treatment, and this process would probably be separate from processes involving treatments. Therefore, the user recording information about treatments will interact with the Treatment class, which will in turn connect to DoctorPersons and PatientPersons, and the user in this case would probably not interact directly with these two objects. Therefore, we can begin to use scenarios to indicate which users interact with which classes of objects, and we can begin to define some of the temporal requirements of the system interaction.

No custom methods are required for these system requirements. The sequence diagram modeling the scenario for recording a treatment is shown in Figure 7.5.

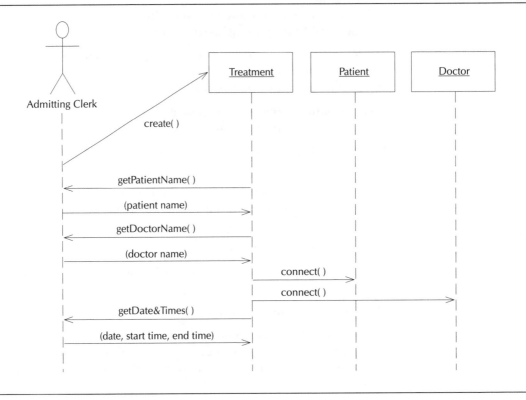

Figure 7.5   Sequence diagram for Add New Treatment scenario

▌ Inheritance from a Class That Is Not Abstract

The generalization/specialization hierarchy can also become more complex. Sometimes a general class includes objects and is also specialized into subclasses that also include objects. For example, consider the requirements for a system that records information about customers of a dive shop. The dive shop sells equipment and supplies, and it also rents diving equipment and boats. The class diagram for a system that just stores information about these customers is shown in Figure 7.6.

Customer is a class that includes the customer's name, address, and phone number. This information is stored for all customers. However, some customers rent diving equipment, and these customers have a diving certificate number and a certificate date. Other customers rent boats, and these customers have a boating safety course completion number and completion date. Therefore, the dive shop has three types of customers, and two of the types of customers are specialized types of a general class of customer.

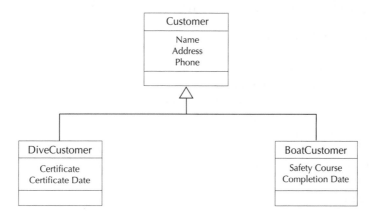

Figure 7.6   Generalization/specialization hierarchy for the Dive Shop (Customer is not an abstract class)

The capabilities of the system can be seen by using the "object think" approach:

I am a Customer (who just purchases supplies).

>I know my Name, Address, and Phone Number.

>I know how to do all of the standard things.

I am a DiveCustomer (who also purchases supplies).

>I am a special type of Customer.

>I know my Certificate number and Certificate Date.

>Since I am a special type of Customer, I also know my Name, Address, and Phone.

>I know how to create myself. And when I do, I add values for the Certificate Number and Certificate Date plus values for Name, Address, and Phone, attributes I inherit from my general class.

I am a BoatCustomer (who also purchases supplies).

>I am a special type of Customer.

>I know my Safety Course and Completion Date.

>Since I am a special type of Customer, I also know my Name, Address, and Phone.

>I know how to create myself. And when I do, I require values for the Safety Course and Completion Date plus values for Name, Address, and Phone, attributes I inherit from my general class.

▌ Generalization/Specialization with Multiple Inheritance

The dive shop example can be expanded to the case where some customers are both dive customers and boat customers. In fact, some customers who dive always rent a boat. The generalization/specialization hierarchy in the previous example would require two objects with some redundancy to handle this case. Figure 7.7 shows the class diagram that includes an additional class, named Dive&BoatCustomer, which appears to solve the problem. Dive&BoatCustomers inherit all of the attributes of a DiveCustomer. Additionally, they inherit all of the attributes of a BoatCustomer. This type of situation is often called **multiple inheritance**, because the objects in the class inherit attributes and services from multiple classes.

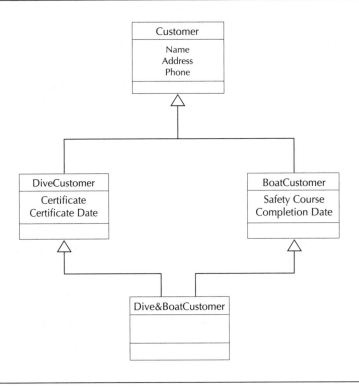

Figure 7.7   Multiple inheritance

The Dive&BoatCustomer class symbol does not list any attributes, yet it is a class that contains objects. Actual Dive&BoatCustomer objects have seven attributes, three from Customer, two from DiveCustomer, and two from BoatCustomer. Although there are no unique attributes, there is a unique collection of attributes. Using "object think:"

I am a Dive&BoatCustomer.

> I am a special type of DiveCustomer.

> I am a special type of BoatCustomer.

> I don't have any unique attributes, but when I create myself, I require values for Name, Address, and Phone, attributes I inherit from Customer; Certificate Number and Certificate Date, attributes I inherit from DiveCustomer; and Safety Course and Completion Date, attributes I inherit from Boat Customer.

> I am tempted to add two values for Name, Address, and Phone, because I inherit these same attributes from two classes. But I am not stupid!

One reason we have provided this example of multiple inheritance is to show how an analyst might uncover more information about the user's work context that requires refining the model. However, this example also shows that the generalization/specialization hierarchy, if not composed of relatively constant or stable classes, can lead to implementation problems. It works best when an object in a special class will always remain a member of that class, for example, a boat customer always remains a boat customer. Unfortunately, in this case, a customer might become a boat customer at any time, and a boat customer might become a dive customer. The resulting system would have to process these changes by deleting one object and then adding another. We will show another way of modeling this in the case study in Chapter 9.

Another solution to this problem would be to model the customer class by using the concept of the roles they play. Roles are a somewhat advanced modeling concept, which we will not discuss in this book.

As a general rule of thumb, you should be on the alert if you have created a generalization/specialization hierarchy with multiple inheritance and you can trace the superclasses back up the hierarchy to a common class, as in the example above. Most likely you have created an unstable generalization/specialization structure, and you should probably try to model the problem in a different way.

Another issue is whether or not multiple inheritance should be allowed at all, and if allowed, how it should be handled. This is still an unresolved issue among developers. Several object-oriented programming languages do not allow multiple inheritance at all. During analysis we might, however, still want to show it on the initial versions of the class diagram if this seems the logical way to classify objects. At a later stage, we might have to change the model to get rid of multiple inheritance (by allowing redundancy, for example).

Whole-Part Relationships

Whole-part relationships, along with generalization/specialization relationships, were described in Chapter 2 as ways people naturally organize information and define concepts. In Chapter 4, whole-part relationships were defined as object relationships in which one object has a particularly strong association with other objects, which are really its parts. In this section, we present a few examples of whole-part relationships. Again, these are relatively simple models, but whole-part relationships are often important in more complex models.

Since whole-part hierarchies include particularly strong relationships, where one object might need to know about its "parts," and since people might naturally define an object based on its parts, defining a whole-part relationship in a class diagram can increase the clarity and precision of the model. It can also reduce the need for detailed scenarios when defining the capabilities of the system.

A whole-part relationship in a class diagram might be used whenever the relationship among objects is based upon the concept of an object and its (physical) parts, a container and its contents, or a collection and its members. Therefore, object relationships that might be designated "is made of" or "contains" or "includes" might indicate a whole-part hierarchy. The terms aggregation and composition are used for whole-part relationships in UML.

In Chapter 6, we used the requirements for a videotape collector to illustrate simple class diagrams. The relationship between a Video object and VideoItems was described as a one-to-many mandatory relationship. This relationship might also be thought of as a whole-part hierarchy: each Video "contains" or "includes" many VideoItems.

Another example of a whole-part hierarchy is the relationship between a specific college at a university and the faculty who teach in the college. The College can be thought of as "containing" or "including" Faculty. Figure 7.8 shows these two examples. The symbol for a whole-part relationship is a diamond on the line connecting the two classes.

In these examples, the whole-part relationship can help to clarify the meaning of the classes of objects. Indeed, a college might be *defined as* a collection of faculty members, and a faculty member might be *defined as* someone who is associated with a college. It is difficult to think of one without thinking of the other. Using the "object think" approach:

I am a College.

Naturally, I know my Name and current Dean.

Naturally, I can create myself and all of that.

But let me tell you more about myself:

Basically, I am a collection of Faculty Members.

I am a Faculty Member.

Naturally, I know my Name, Rank, and Specialty.

Naturally, I can create myself and all of that.

But let me tell you more about myself:

Basically, I am someone who teaches at a College.

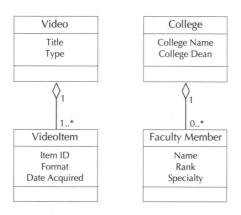

Figure 7.8   Whole-part relationships (aggregation) with cardinality/multiplicity indicated

▌ A More Complex Whole-Part Hierarchy

The dive shop, discussed earlier in this chapter, includes a more complex whole-part hierarchy. One item that the customer can rent is a boat. However, a boat in this context is not really one item. A boat is a collection of parts. To fully understand the requirements for the dive shop system, the analyst must fully understand what is rented in the work context of the dive shop.

At this dive shop, a Boat Assembly, not a boat, is rented. One Boat Assembly "contains" a boat hull, a motor, and a trailer. Another Boat Assembly contains a boat hull and two motors, but no trailer. A third Boat Assembly contains a boat hull and a trailer, but no motor. It is important to the dive shop that these Boat Assemblies "know" what they include. The Boat Assemblies are permanent "packages" whose parts stay together and never get rented separately.

For the dive shop, it is important to know about the details of each boat assembly rented. First of all, they need to know what they are renting to determine the rental price. Second, they need to know what was rented so they can be sure they get the complete boat assembly back again!

Figure 7.9 shows a whole-part hierarchy that models these requirements for the dive shop. Using the "object think" approach:

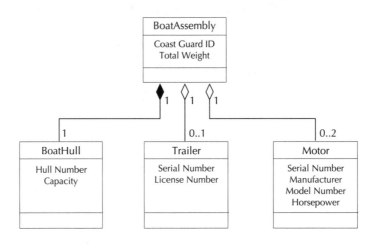

Figure 7.9   Whole-part relationships (composition and aggregation) for a boat assembly for the Dive Shop

I am a Boat Assembly.

Let me tell you about myself:

Basically, I am a collection of parts.

I definitely have a Boat Hull.

I might have a Trailer.

I might have a Motor, or even two.

The requirements for the system can be clarified by thinking through some scenarios. The whole-part hierarchy is useful here because we can assume that the Boat Assembly "knows" all about its parts. Therefore, the scenario for adding a new Boat Assembly can be streamlined, as shown below.

1. **Event: A new boat assembly is purchased for rental by the dive shop. Use Case: Add new boat assembly, main scenario**

The user sends a message to Boat Assembly asking it to add a new Boat Assembly object.

Boat Assembly knows it needs the Coast Guard ID and Total Weight to add a Boat Assembly object, so it asks the user for those values.

The user supplies the requested values.

Boat Assembly then adds a Boat Assembly object.

Boat Assembly also knows that it is a collection of parts, and it knows that it has one Boat Hull. Therefore, Boat Assembly will ask the user for the Hull Number and Capacity of its Boat Hull.

The user supplies the Boat Hull values.

Boat Assembly asks Boat Hull to add a new Boat Hull object.

Boat Assembly knows it might include one Trailer, so it asks the user if it includes a Trailer. If so, it asks for the values for Serial Number and License Number.

The user supplies the Trailer values.

Boat Assembly asks Trailer to add a new Trailer object.

Boat Assembly knows it might include one or more Motors, so it asks the user if it includes Motors. If so, for each motor, it asks the user for the Serial Number, Manufacturer, Model Number, and Horsepower.

The user supplies the Motor values.

Boat Assembly asks Motor to add a Motor object.

In this scenario, we have assumed that Boat Assembly is responsible for getting the required information from the user and then adding the Boat Hull, Trailer, and Motors. This one scenario provides an example of how the strength of a whole-part relationship might be used to assign responsibilities to a class. Boat Assembly is given the responsibility for taking care of assembling its parts so no one else has to worry about the details. But this is just one way that the user might interact with the system. The sequence diagram modeling this scenario is shown in Figure 7.10.

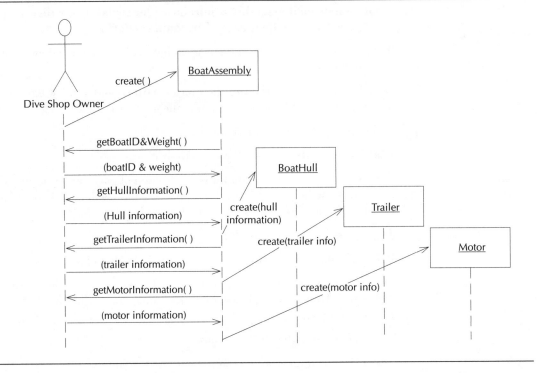

Figure 7.10   Sequence diagram for Add New Boat Assembly scenario

▌ Key Term

multiple inheritance

▌ Review Questions

1. What can one class inherit from another class?

2. What symbol in the class diagram indicates a generalization/specialization hierarchy?

3. What is the difference between a class with its name written in italics and a class with its name written with ordinary letters?

4. What is a nonexhaustive generalization/specialization hierarchy?

5. What is multiple inheritance?

6. Why is the multiple inheritance example for the dive shop a potential problem?

7. Explain why whole-part hierarchies contain object relationships but generalization/specialization hierarchies do not.

8. What are the advantages of using whole-part hierarchies in the class diagram?

▮ Discussion Question

1. Compare/contrast generalization/specialization hierarchies and whole-part hierarchies in terms of:
   a. inheritance
   b. object relationships and multiplicity
   c. the benefits resulting from the way users think about their work
   d. the benefits resulting from reuse

▮ Exercises

1. Create a class diagram that classifies types of animals treated by the veterinarian discussed in Chapter 3. Include reasonable attributes.

2. Create a class diagram that classifies types of computers (see Chapter 2 exercise). If the "system" only includes information about one computer (a personal computer), how many objects are there in the system?

3. Create a class diagram that shows a computer and its parts (see Chapter 2 exercise). If the "system" only includes information about one computer and its parts, how many objects are there in the system?

4. In the example of a Treatment for a PatientPerson (Figure 7.4), each Treatment might be associated with a TreatmentType. Expand the class diagram to show TreatmentType and its relationship to Treatment. Then expand the model further to show a whole-part hierarchy for Treatment Type, because each TreatmentType contains or includes specific things (e.g., supplies, medicines, and procedures).

8

Object-Oriented System Development Life Cycles

- Introduction

- An Overview of System Development Life Cycles

- What Is a System Development Methodology?

- The Need for Object-Oriented System Development Methodologies

- What Is Object-Oriented Analysis?

- What Is Object-Oriented Design?

- What Is Object-Oriented Implementation?

Introduction

Up to this point we have discussed object-oriented concepts and modeling. This chapter focuses more specifically on the system development process. When you have completed this chapter, you should understand the similarities and differences between traditional system development and object-oriented development. First, the system development life cycle will be discussed and related to object-oriented development. Next, we will discuss the need for object-oriented system development methodologies and the general trends and features of such methodologies. Finally, we will provide a brief overview of object-oriented analysis (OOA), object-oriented design (OOD), and object-oriented implementation using object-oriented programming (OOP). When you have completed this chapter, you should know common general features of life cycle models for object-oriented development and understand what system development methodologies generally include and the specific requirements for object-oriented methodologies.

An Overview of System Development Life Cycles

The quality of developed information systems increases considerably when the development process is carefully managed. The **system development life cycle (SDLC)** is a widely used framework for organizing and managing the process. A system development life cycle typically defines phases that are completed by the project team as they move from the beginning to the end of the development project. The term life cycle is used because every information development project has a beginning and eventually an ending. Between these points in time, the project "lives" in one form or another.

Each project phase includes specific tasks, or steps, that the development team should follow, and each task or set of tasks usually results in a completed product, or **deliverable**. A deliverable is something finished or completed, often a finished document or model describing something about the system, or a completed part of the system itself.

The first phase defines what the new system is intended to accomplish and how the project will be organized, and it is generally called **system planning**. The second phase involves investigating and documenting in detail what the system actually should do to accomplish what is intended, and it is generally called **system analysis**. At the end of the systems analysis phase, the project team should have detailed and hopefully accurate ideas of the requirements for the system. Once the requirements are fully understood and agreed to, the team begins specifying in detail how they will implement the system using specific technology, and this phase is generally called **system design**.

When the system design details are complete, the team begins creating the actual system. When programming and testing are complete, the finished system is put in use, and hopefully it begins providing the intended benefits. The process of creating the system and putting it into actual use is often called the **implementation phase**. After implementation, needed improvements (and fixes) are provided over a long period of time, and this is generally called the **maintenance phase**. The maintenance phase lasts for as long as the system is being used.

There are many variations of the system development life cycle. For example, some life cycles use different terms for the phases (or use the term stage instead of phase), and some life cycles divide the development process into a set of smaller phases.

The phases can be completed sequentially, although in practice they often overlap. For example, some project team members might be working on a task that is part of one phase while other team members have moved ahead to work on tasks in the next phase.

There has been a move away from a sequential or waterfall approach to a more **iterative approach**, whereby previous parts of the life cycle can be revisited for further enhancement. The waterfall approach was (seemingly) good from a management perspective because it provided predictability and a foundation for measuring progress. It did not, however, provide for the fact that users rarely are able to specify clear and complete requirements up front. "Frozen" requirements specifications did usually not meet the real needs of the users and left them quite dissatisfied with the resultant system. An iterative approach acknowledges that users and developers learn about the real underlying requirements as they progress in the development process, and it allows for that learning to influence the development process and the final result.

In addition to the requirements issue and the move to an iterative approach, most of the important changes over the years in the system development life cycle have occurred because of the need to speed up the development process. Several tools and techniques are commonly used, such as **joint application design (JAD)**, **time boxing**, **prototyping**, and **computer-aided system or software engineering (CASE)**. Joint application design means that a group of developers and users meet intensively until most of the analysis and even some of the design is complete. Time boxing means arranging the project so that there will be delivery of certain significant parts of the project at the end of each time box, which is a predefined period of time, often 6 to 8 weeks. This ensures a continued focus on delivery and the most significant part of the deliverable. Prototyping means that the developers create a working model of parts of the system during analysis or design for the users to try out. CASE tools provide the developer with automated support for creating analysis and design models, and they often generate program statements directly from the design models. Use of these tools and techniques are often collectively referred to as **RAD (rapid application development)**. They allow system development to proceed more iteratively and with life cycle phases often completed in parallel rather than in sequence.

Large project size and long elapsed time from project initialization to system delivery are well-known factors that characterize projects in trouble. To limit the size of projects and shorten the time it takes to provide the users with at least some useful functionality, approaches like **incremental development** (divide the system into parts and build the system in a piecemeal fashion, with the most important part first) and **evolutionary development** (develop a limited version first and add new features and functionality later) are becoming increasingly popular.

Object-oriented development should also follow a defined system development life cycle, and the phases themselves are really the same. System *planning* is required, system *analysis* is required, system *design* is required, *implementation* is required, and *maintenance* is required. As with traditional development, JAD, time boxing, prototyping, and CASE are just as desirable with object-oriented development. Also, the life cycle phases can be, and usually are, completed more in parallel, with lots of iteration. Development is incremental, with increments based on the use cases. Those use cases that are most important, either because they provide the most value to the user or because they represent the most risk, are worked on first. Such an approach is often referred to as being **use case driven**.

Although the distinctions between the analysis, design, and implementation phases are still important and useful from a conceptual point of view, in practice the distinctions get blurred, and object-oriented system development typically proceeds something like this:

1. The system definition and scope are decided on.
2. Some of the key use cases are identified and modeled.
3. Some of the key classes of objects are identified and modeled.
4. Some of the key scenarios are explored and modeled.
5. Partial requirements models are finalized.
6. Some interface objects and operating environment objects are added for design models.
7. The key scenarios are implemented and tested using object-oriented programming.
8. The initial implementation is evaluated by end users.
9. The initial implementation is improved (the requirements, the design, and the programming). Additional use cases and classes of objects that are required are investigated and modeled, and the cycle (steps 2–8) repeats.
10. A complete, tested, and approved system is available for use.

In summary, some of the main features of modern life cycles for object-oriented development are that they are prototype-based, iterative, incremental, and use case driven.

What Is a System Development Methodology?

An overview of the system development life cycle provides us with a general understanding of what system development is all about. However, a generic life cycle does not give us much guidance on how to actually carry out system development. To help us develop quality information systems in a timely and manageable way, we need more complete system development **methodologies**.

A system development methodology defines the process and sequence of tasks that need to be completed when developing a system, along with recommended techniques for completing the tasks. It generally has two main components, related to what and how. One is the **process component**, explaining what tasks to do and when to do them, spelling out the life cycle to follow and the general project management approaches to be used. The other is the **techniques** component, describing the techniques that could or should be used for the tasks at hand.

We will use the terms **method** and methodology interchangeably, but sometimes the term method is used when only part of the system development life cycle is considered and the term methodology is used when the entire life cycle is considered.

In any method many different techniques might be used. For example, graphical modeling techniques, such as data flow diagramming and object modeling, and information gathering techniques, such as JAD sessions and structured interviews, might be recommended. The same technique might be used in many different methods, and different methods might use different techniques for similar tasks.

What is needed in a system development method varies widely with the projects undertaken. One decisive factor is the number of people involved. In small projects, the main modeling techniques to be used are the most important aspect of the method. As the project size increases and more people are involved, the need for a comprehensive method with a clearly defined process increases rapidly. Another decisive factor is the criticality of the project. If we are developing software for a patient monitoring system in a hospital where program bugs might be life threatening, the need for a well-defined process is greater than if we are developing software in which bugs and malfunctions would merely cause some inconvenience.

Ideally, a comprehensive method should provide a clear work breakdown structure that divides the development effort into phases, steps, and tasks. The method should tell us about the sequence of tasks: which can be done in parallel, which can be skipped under certain circumstances, and so on. The method should also tell us what is required as input to each task and what the output or deliverables should be. Further, it should tell us which techniques to use to complete each task. At the same time, the method should be flexible and adaptable to the project at hand by allowing the deleting, rearranging, and combining of steps and tasks. Methodologies without such flexibility can be overly bureaucratic and stifle creativity and performance.

Presently, we can observe two opposing trends in the methodology world. One advocates a clearly defined and tightly managed process, emphasizing rigor, predictability, and engineering-like development. This approach is exemplified by the work of the SEI (software engineering institute) at Carnegie Mellon University and its **Capability Maturity Model (CMM)** framework (Paulk et. al. 1995).

Others, such as James Highsmith (1999) in his book *Adaptive Software Development* and Kent Beck (1999) through his **Extreme Programming method**, advocate methodology minimalism and maximum freedom on the part of the developers to adapt their approaches according to the needs of the project. In modern development, requirements change quickly and the pressure to deliver software rapidly to support the business in a highly competitive world is high. Too much method adherence and rigidity might slow down the project. A basic premise is, therefore, that you should not use more method prescription than strictly necessary.

Both approaches have merits, but also potential drawbacks. The flip side of a rigorous approach is that it could lead to stifling bureaucracy and too long delivery times. The flip side of an adaptive and flexible approach is that it could lead to an unmanageable hacking type of development.

■ The Need for Object-Oriented System Development Methodologies

System development methodologies supposedly help organizations develop quality information systems in a timely and manageable way. Moving to an object-oriented approach to system development does not reduce the need for a methodology to follow. It does, however, change what the content of the methodology should be. Because the underlying thinking in object-oriented development is so different, the differences have to be reflected in the methodology that is used.

In an object-oriented methodology, there should be the same amount of process guidance as in structured methodologies, if required, but an object-oriented methodology should be geared toward developing software using object-oriented techniques and technologies. Object-oriented models, object-oriented database management systems, and object-oriented programming languages should be incorporated. Object-oriented development encourages using prototyping with use case driven incremental systems delivery and extensive reuse of existing classes. An object-oriented method must allow for and facilitate prototyping and reuse.

Although UML has emerged as an accepted modeling standard, there is no recognized methodology standard, and there are a number of UML-based methods available. One of the best known on the market today is the **Rational Unified Process (RUP)** put together by Booch, Jacobson, and Rumbaugh (1999). A good overview of RUP is found in Kruchten's book *The Rational Unified Process—An Introduction* (Kruchten 1999).

A system development methodology defines a sequence of tasks that are completed when developing a system, along with recommended techniques for completing each task. It thus provides detailed content and structure for the life cycle phases. We do not follow a specific methodology in this book, but we do demonstrate the main activities and models used with most UML-based object-oriented analysis methods, in the following chapter.

What Is Object-Oriented Analysis?

Object-oriented analysis usually involves four main activities, shown in Figure 8.1, that produce a complete requirements model. These activities are:

- Create the system definition.
- Define system functionality through use cases and scenarios.
- Build the class diagram and the interaction models.
- Finalize the analysis documentation.

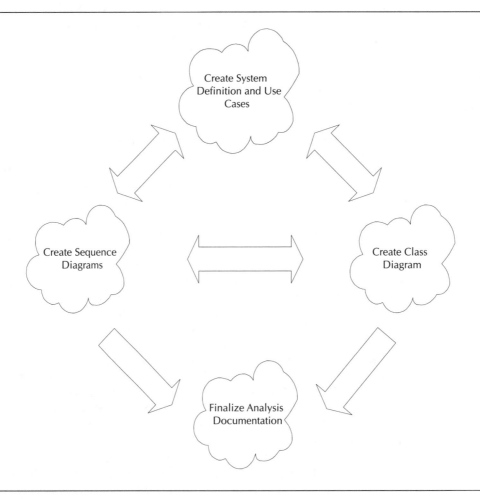

Figure 8.1   The object-oriented analysis process

The system definition and the initial use case model are created first. The class diagram and interaction models are then developed in parallel with necessary changes to the use case model. The final analysis documentation is assembled and thoroughly reviewed with the end users of the system.

The analysis phase does not really end so abruptly, however. Design and implementation activities are often done in parallel with the analysis activities. In use case driven development, design and implementation of the most important use cases and scenarios are carried out before more analysis activities are carried out related to the rest of the scenarios.

Before any detailed analysis or modeling is begun, the analyst should create a definition of the proposed system. The **system definition** includes a statement of the objectives of the system development project, including a preliminary definition of the system scope. The system definition is usually a short, written description. The **objectives** are statements that define the expected benefits of the system. The system **scope** defines the boundary of the system and describes what the system will be used for and the main users.

The system definition might have been part of a strategic IS planning effort or might be done as a separate task prior to starting a project. There is nothing particularly object-oriented about this activity, and any successful approach that an organization is presently using would also work for object-oriented development.

After the system definition is agreed to and the main use cases have been identified, two major activities in the object-oriented analysis process are usually carried out in parallel, with lots of iteration:

- Build a class diagram with the capability to satisfy the requirements.
- Develop scenarios through sequence diagrams.

The systems analyst carefully studies the user's work context, and through JAD sessions, interviews, and other research begins building a model of the classes of objects that are part of the problem domain of the system users. The analyst adds a few classes, models a few scenarios, and possibly sketches a few sequence diagrams and statechart diagrams. Much discussion and revision goes on until the analyst has a good understanding of all of the classes and scenarios that seem to define the requirements for the system. In many cases the analyst can find some of the required classes in existing systems or class libraries and use the class description in the object model.

Eventually, the models are completed and reviewed with the users, although with object-oriented analysis it is not always clear when or if the model is complete, as we will discuss below. Object-oriented analysis, then, differs from structured analysis in the focus of the analyst (on use cases, scenarios, classes and objects, and interactions) and in the types of models produced (use case diagram, class diagram, sequence diagrams, and statecharts).

What Is Object-Oriented Design?

Object-oriented design, like traditional system design, is the phase that takes the requirements model and uses it to develop more physical models that show how the new system will actually be implemented. With traditional structured design, the structure chart and a database schema are produced to document the set of program modules required and the database structure that the modules access. The data flow diagrams (and supporting documentation) from the analysis phase might be revised somewhat to show a more physical model of system processes, but eventually the data flow diagrams must be converted to a different form of model (the structure chart). The user interface is designed, controls are designed, and technical issues affecting implementation are resolved. The transition from structured analysis to structured design is quite abrupt, and some information contained in the requirements model is often lost or distorted when the requirements model is translated into a design model.

Object-oriented design takes the requirements model produced during the analysis phase and adds to it. The same models and model notation are used, so there is no translation process from model to model. Sometimes more attributes are added or more methods are added. The user interface is designed by adding interface classes and by adding references to specific devices and interface objects in the scenarios and sequence diagrams. Controls and data access considerations are addressed, but again objects that provide these functions are added to the models.

Classes required by the system might already exist in class libraries in the development environment, so the design phase might involve searching for and finding existing classes as well as designing new ones.

Because the same models and model notation are used in both analysis and design, it is usually difficult to define exactly when analysis ends and design begins. Different object-oriented development approaches define different cutoff points. However, the ending and beginning are less important because the models produced during analysis are added to and refined during design. Since much detail is added to the model in the design phase, additional notation to convey the detail might be needed in the models. UML also defines additional graphical models that tie in with the main models to convey design details.

What Is Object-Oriented Implementation?

Object-oriented implementation is the life cycle phase in which the object model begun during analysis and completed during design is turned into a set of interacting objects in the computer system. Object-oriented programming languages are designed to allow the programmer to directly create classes of objects in the computer system that correspond to classes of objects in the models. These include both problem domain classes and interface classes and operating environment classes. Usually it is necessary to use a separate database management system along with the object-oriented programming language, and these are called object-oriented database management systems (OODBMS). When implementing the system, the system developers are still thinking in terms of objects and classes, they are still looking at models of objects and classes, and they are still interpreting scenarios and sequence diagrams that document object behavior.

■ Key Terms

Capability Maturity Model (CMM)

computer-aided system or software engineering (CASE)

evolutionary development

extreme programming method

implementation phase

incremental development

iterative approach

joint application design (JAD)

maintenance phase

method

methodologies (synonym methods)

process component

prototyping

rapid application development (RAD)

Rational Unified Process (RUP)

system analysis phase

system definition objectives

system design phase

system development life cycle (SDLC)

system planning phase

techniques

time boxing

use case driven approach

■ Review Questions

1. What are the "generic" phases of the systems development life cycle?

2. What are JAD, prototyping, time boxing, and CASE tools?

3. What are the steps usually followed when the iterative approach to object-oriented development is used?

4. What is a system development methodology?

5. What are the four main activities of object-oriented analysis?

6. What characterizes use case driven system development?

7. Which activities of object-oriented analysis are done iteratively?

8. What is incremental development? Evolutionary development?

9. What are the main activities of object-oriented design and object-oriented implementation?

Exercise and Discussion Question

1. Research and then discuss whether the system development life cycle for the object-oriented approach is virtually the same as or completely different from the systems development life cycle for the traditional structured approach in terms of:

   a. the names of the phases

   b. the objectives of the phases

   c. the sequence of the phases

   d. the activities of the analyst during the phases

   e. the models or deliverables produced during the phases

   f. the iteration across phases

References

Beck, K. *Extreme Programming Explained: Embrace Change*. Reading, Massachusetts: Addison-Wesley, 1999.

Highsmith, J. *Adaptive Software Development: A Collaborative Approach to Managing Complex Systems*. New York, New York: Dorset House, 1999.

Jacobsen, I., Booch, G., and Rumbaugh, J. *The Unified Software Development Process*. Reading, Massachusetts: Addison-Wesley, 1999.

Kruchten, P. *The Rational Unified Process—An Introduction*. Reading, Massachusetts: Addison-Wesley, 1999.

Paulk, M., Weber, C., and Curtis, B. *The Capability Maturity Model: Guidelines for Improving the Software Process* (SEI Series in Software Engineering). Reading, Massachusetts: Addison-Wesley, 1995.

An Object-Oriented Analysis Case Study of Dick's Dive 'n' Thrive

9

Introduction

In Chapters 6 and 7, we described requirements models through examples that included use case diagrams, class diagrams, and sequence diagrams. The examples were fairly simple, although most of the key types of model components were shown and explained. In this chapter, we will discuss the process followed when developing the requirements model, and we will use a more elaborate case study. The process followed to create the requirements model is what object-oriented analysis is all about. The case study is the equipment rental system of Dick's Dive 'n' Thrive, the dive shop used in some of the examples in Chapter 7.

When you have completed this chapter, you should be able to describe the object-oriented analysis process and have a good understanding of the way the requirements models are developed. Additionally, you should understand how the features of UML models, demonstrated in Chapter 6 and Chapter 7, fit together in a larger model.

An Overview of the Object-Oriented Analysis Process

As explained in Chapter 8, the object-oriented analysis process involves four main activities. These activities are: create the system definition and decide the system's main functionality through use cases, build the class diagram, develop scenarios and corresponding sequence diagrams, and finalize the analysis documentation.

The system definition is created first. After the system definition is agreed to, the most important use cases are identified. Use cases provide a natural way of dividing the system into manageable units. The objective is to identify what the system must do for the user to complete the required work tasks.

The next two major activities in the object-oriented analysis process are usually carried out in parallel, with lots of iteration:

- Build a class diagram with the capability to satisfy the requirements.
- Develop scenarios through sequence diagrams.

The final analysis documentation is then assembled and thoroughly reviewed with the end users of the system.

In Chapters 6 and 7, the results of the two major steps were presented in the video collector examples and the dive shop examples. That is, the scenarios with accompanying sequence diagrams and the final class diagram were described. This chapter is concerned with the analysis process used to define all of the information contained in the requirements models. There are many different approaches used for the object-oriented analysis process, especially for defining system requirements. The approach used in this chapter draws on several leading methods and is fairly generic.

We will walk through an example showing how the process of developing the three types of models might unfold. In practice, there will be (at least) one main scenario for each use case and a number of secondary scenarios reflecting special cases, error handling, etc. All the main scenarios and some of the secondary ones will normally be explored and documented through sequence diagrams. Because the procedure will be similar for all of the use cases, we will only show how the main scenario and some of the secondary scenarios for the main use case are developed and how they influence the development of the class diagram. In practice, we will often go through one or a couple of the use cases in a first iteration and implement those to create a working prototype before we move on to explore more of the use cases. How many iterations and how many use cases to take on in each iteration depend on the total number of use cases and their complexity.

◼ Dick's Dive 'n' Thrive

Our case study example is based on the equipment rental system needed by Dick's Dive 'n' Thrive, DDT for short. DDT is a small business that rents diving equipment and boats. They also sell equipment and organize diving trips. The customers have been extremely pleased with the diving trips. Write-ups in diving magazines and word of mouth among diving devotees have generated tremendous growth for DDT. Dick is a great diver, but not much of a manager. The business has not been able to handle the growth.

Dick realizes that new business procedures and controls have to be established, especially for the equipment rental part of the business. He thinks a computer system is probably needed, so he decided to ask a small consulting firm to help him develop one. The consultants suggest using object-oriented development, initially focusing on the rental operations only, where the greatest problems and opportunities are. The consultants wrote up a proposal for the development project, defining the scope as equipment rental operations, listing the primary objectives as better control of rental inventory and better tracking of rental contracts for customers. The system is also expected to improve customer service and reduce costs by automating the rental contract process.

◼ Identifying Use Cases and Building the Use Case Diagram

The consultants need to understand more about the equipment rental business, and they conduct a brainstorming session with Dick to identify the main use cases. They start out by identifying the most important business events.

The most important business event is *a customer rents something*. No detailed event analysis is required to reveal that. Customers also *return rented equipment*. It was also apparent that *DDT acquires new equipment*. After interviewing DDT staff, other events also surfaced: *equipment is discarded* (because of wear and tear, age, accidents and so on), and sometimes *equipment is temporarily taken out of service* (for maintenance or repair). Naturally, there might be many more events, but only the important or typical events need to be identified early on.

The events translate into a list of use cases:

- Rent equipment
- Return equipment
- Add new equipment
- Discard equipment
- Suspend equipment

They also realize that the system might provide them with different types of reports that might help with managing the business, and without going into detail about which reports will be needed, they decide to include "generate reports" as an additional use case.

The consultants also try to figure out who will be interacting with the system, and Dick mentioned the names of the persons who will be involved in the different use cases. When generating the use case diagram, the consultants will not be concerned with actual people's names, but rather with the roles they play. From the discussion, it soon emerges that there are two main roles involved: the desk manager and the service manager.

Based on this background material, the consultants developed the use case diagram shown in Figure 9.1, which was fully discussed with Dick and the other users and agreed upon as a useful first cut.

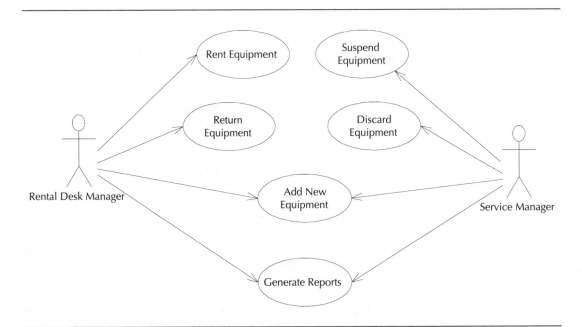

Figure 9.1   Initial Use Case Diagram for Dick's Dive 'n' Thrive

■ Developing Initial Scenarios and Initial Classes

Based on the initial discussions and the use case diagram, the consultants are ready to start developing the scenarios and building the class diagram. They will choose one or two use cases that are considered to be the most important and develop those in parallel with the class diagram.

Procedure for Building the Class Diagram

Most object-oriented analysis methods suggest a general sequence to follow when building the class diagram. Most start by defining the main classes that are required in the system. Then the classes are expanded and refined and additional details are added to the model. The main idea is that one class is not identified, refined, and completed before moving on to the next class. Instead, general information is gathered and included in the model as the information surfaces. Then, more details are added later once the overall class structure begins to take shape. Throughout the process, anything and everything is subject to change.

The steps for developing the class diagram followed in this chapter are:

1. Identify problem domain classes.
2. Identify generalization/specialization hierarchies and whole-part hierarchies to refine problem domain classes.
3. Identify the important attributes.
4. Identify additional association relationships.
5. Identify custom methods of classes.
6. Specify time-dependent behavior of objects.

Remember that, although it is necessary to present these steps in sequence, the steps are not completed in a sequential fashion. Much iteration between different tasks will take place. The example in this chapter illustrates the steps of the process, and some guidelines for completing the steps are included in the example.

Finding Initial Problem Domain Classes

The consultants started by identifying classes of objects that are involved in rental operations. Finding objects and classes is usually a key activity in object-oriented modeling. Authors dealing with object-oriented analysis offer different approaches to this. In practice, knowledge of the business, rules of thumb (heuristics), and experience seem to play an important role.

Looking for nouns in written descriptions of the business is one approach that usually reveals some important classes, so an existing brief description of DDT's rental operations was used by the consultants as a starting point:

> "*Customers* can rent *diving equipment* and *boats* from DDT. When the customer has seen what is available and made a decision about what to rent, a rental agreement, or *contract*, is produced and signed."

By looking for nouns, the consultants could see that *customer*, *diving equipment*, *boat*, and *contract* all are prime candidates for problem domain classes. Part of the class diagram began to take form, as shown in Figure 9.2.

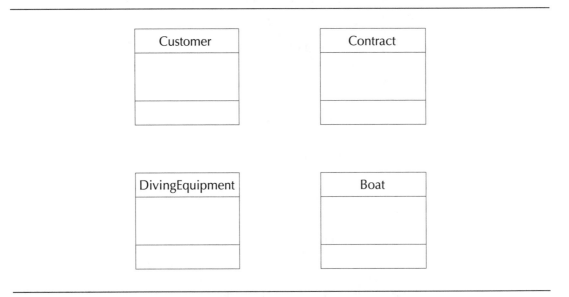

Figure 9.2   Four initial classes for Dick's Dive'n' Thrive

First Cut Scenarios for the Main Use Case

The consultants still needed to understand more about the equipment rental business. To confirm that the initial classes in Figure 9-2 are good classes to use in the model, an initial picture of the way the classes of objects in the system will be used was developed by looking at the business events and use cases. This is done to ensure that the class diagram being developed is capable of handling and responding correctly to the use cases. The most important business event discussed above is *a customer rents something*, and the use case that results is *rent equipment*.

One important thing to look for when exploring the use case when a customer rents something is the class that should be responsible for much of the processing.

When Dick talked about his business, he kept emphasizing the rental *contract*. The contract seemed to be the central concern of the system. Hence, the consultants decided to assign the responsibility for rental processing to the class named Contract.

It was soon evident that there is a difference between handling new and existing customers, and there is often a difference between handling boat equipment and diving equipment. Although UML provides notation for showing logic in complex interactions, it generally pays to keep each sequence diagram simple by defining separate scenarios for each situation. So, at least four scenarios and four sequence diagrams are required to model the interactions involved:

- Rent boat to existing customer
- Rent boat to new customer
- Rent diving equipment to existing customer
- Rent diving equipment to new customer

The first scenario was written at a high level to explore the classes involved and the interactions in the system as follows:

1. **Event: Customer rents something**

   Use Case: Rent equipment
   Scenario: Rent boat to existing customer

   The user asks Contract to create a new Contract object.

   Contract connects to the correct Customer object.

   Contract connects to the Boat object, and gets some information about the amount to charge for the rental.

   Contract provides the contract details in whatever form the user might require.

The first scenario was documented with the sequence diagram shown in Figure 9.3. After thinking through and discussing the diagram, the consultants were satisfied that they are on the right track. The next scenario was written to document what happens when a new customer rents a boat. The sequence diagram is shown in Figure 9.4, and the scenario is as follows:

Scenario: Rent boat to new customer

The user asks Contract to create a new Contract object.

Contract knows it needs to create a new Customer object, so it asks Customer to create a new Customer object.

Customer needs information to create itself, so the new Customer object asks the user for name, address, and other information.

The user supplies the requested information, and then Customer supplies the information to Contract.

Contract connects to the Boat object, and gets some information about the amount to charge for the rental.

Contract provides the contract details in whatever form the user might require.

The other two scenarios for this use case are very similar to the ones shown here, and are not shown in this text.

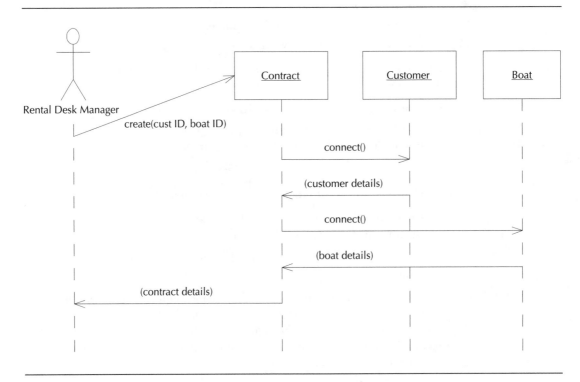

Figure 9.3   Initial sequence diagram for scenario: Rent Boat to Existing Customer

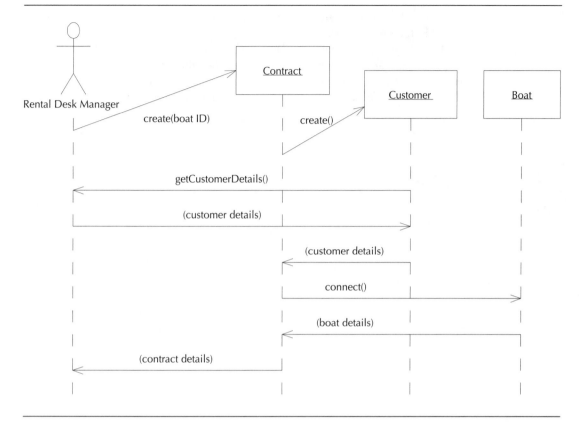

Figure 9.4   Initial sequence diagram for scenario: Rent Boat to New Customer

Refining Scenarios and Classes

The consultants began to refine and expand the classes in the class diagram by looking for potential generalization/specialization hierarchies and whole-part hierarchies, like those discussed in Chapter 7. First they focused on possible generalization/specialization hierarchies, and then they looked for whole-part hierarchies. The order is not important.

Identifying Generalization/Specialization Hierarchies

Either a top-down approach or a bottom-up approach might be used to refine a class into a generalization/specialization hierarchy. The top-down approach takes one class and expands it into specialized subclasses. The bottom-up approach takes specialized classes and creates a general class. Both approaches are demonstrated in the examples that follow.

Two classes in the example, Diving Equipment and Boat, are both types of equipment that are rented. So the consultants thought it was meaningful to create a general class called Rental Equipment, producing the generalization/specialization hierarchy shown in Figure 9.5. This is an example of the bottom-up approach.

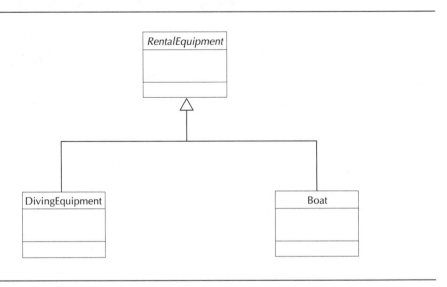

Figure 9.5   Initial rental equipment generalization/specialization hierarchy

The attributes and methods later defined for Rental Equipment will be inherited by the classes Diving Equipment and Boat. If Diving Equipment and Boat are exhaustive classes (i.e., DDT doesn't rent anything but boats and diving equipment), the Rental Equipment class will be an abstract class. This is similar to the example of the generalization/specialization hierarchy that includes the Doctor Person and the Patient Person in Chapter 7, and it is shown in the model by writing the class name in italics. The general class serves as a vehicle for specifying common attributes and methods and possibly reducing the number of object relationships.

The consultants then looked closer at the Diving Equipment class. DDT rents all of the usual diving equipment such as tanks, regulators, weight belts, diving suits, and depth gauges. They then considered whether some types of diving equipment might be more specialized. Was there any type of equipment they needed to store additional information about? Diving suits, for example, come in various sizes, thicknesses, and types (dry and wet). This type of information will not be relevant for all objects in the Diving Equipment class, only for diving suits.

Having attributes that are only relevant for some of the objects in a class indicates that we have a specialized subclass.

Although the specific attributes are not specified at this point, it is still necessary to think about needed attributes ("what the object needs to know") to decide what kind of subclasses to include. Because the consultants were becoming more familiar with the business and the intended use of the system, they had a fairly good idea about the attributes that were needed. So, by thinking about the attributes that are relevant for only some of the objects, they recognized a need for a subclass named Diving Suit, which has been added to the diagram shown in Figure 9.6. This is an example of the top-down approach.

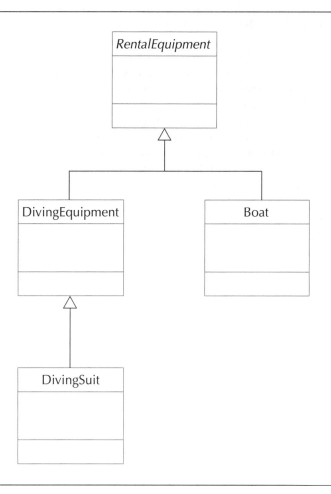

Figure 9.6   Diving suit added as a special type of diving equipment

At a later stage, they might have to refine the Diving Equipment class further, but for now they left it with the one subclass named Diving Suit. This means that every piece of diving equipment DDT rents, except for diving suits, is classified as just diving equipment and can be described with an attribute telling us what type of equipment it is (e.g., tank, regulator, etc.). The diving equipment class has objects (the subclass is not exhaustive). This is captured in the way the class name is written in the model (no italics).

In addition to the methods and attributes that are later specified for it, the Diving Suit class will inherit all specified attributes and methods from Diving Equipment and from Rental Equipment. A Diving Suit *is a* special kind of Diving Equipment, which *is a* special kind of Rental Equipment.

The consultants then took a closer look at DDT's customers. After more discussion with Dick, they concluded that the difference between boat customers and diving customers is significant in DDT's context (for example, because of different licensing and different insurance requirements). Using the top-down approach, they created a classification hierarchy with two subclasses because Dive Customers have different attributes from Boat Customers. This example was explained in Chapter 7.

Dive Customer and Boat Customer are exhaustive subclasses, so there will be no Customer objects, and Customer is an abstract class. This example is slightly different from the example in Chapter 7 because here we are focusing only on rental operations. The consultants also discovered that many customers rent both diving equipment and a boat, so the Dive and Boat Customer class was initially added, as shown in Figure 9.7.

After pondering the model for a while they realized that they had created a generalization/specialization structure that was likely to be unstable (see the discussion in Chapter 7), and they tried to find another way to look at this. Instead of focusing on different types of customers, they realized that the diving-related information could be contained in a class they called a Diving License, and similarly boat-related information could be associated with a Boat License. The Customer object would then be associated with a Diving License object or a Boat License object, or both. These associations are strong relationships in the sense that neither the Boat License nor Dive License objects can exist without a corresponding Customer object. The consultants therefore choose to portray this as whole-part relationships (composition), as shown in Figure 9.8.

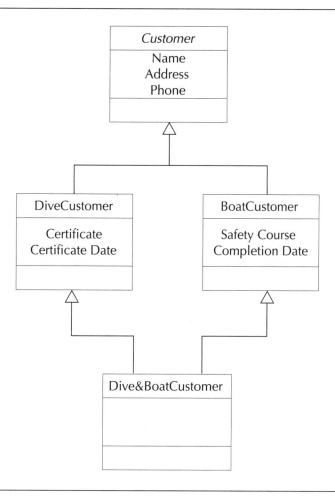

Figure 9.7   Initial customer generalization/specialization hierarchy with multiple inheritance

Notice that in the previous generalization/specialization approach acquiring a new customer would mean adding one new object (either a Dive Customer, a Boat Customer, or a Boat and Dive Customer). In the new approach, acquiring a new Customer would require adding either two objects: a Customer object and Dive License object or a Customer object and Boat License object, or adding three objects: a Customer, a Dive License, and a Boat License.

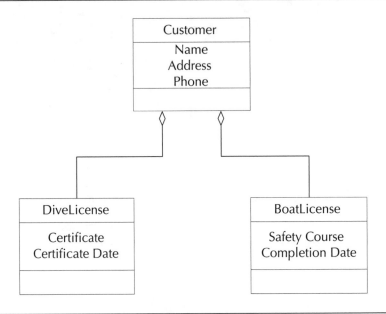

Figure 9.8   Solution showing Customer class associated with Dive License and Boat License classes

Once the Customer class issues were resolved, the consultants again wanted to confirm that they were on the right track, so they looked over the use case and initial scenarios to see if the model was consistent with the needs of the business. They found that a few changes might be made to the scenarios for the *Rent equipment* use case to refine it slightly

■ Identifying Whole-Part Hierarchies

The consultants next looked for potential whole-part hierarchies of importance. A top-down or a bottom-up approach can also be used to define a whole-part hierarchy. Taking a fresh look at the scenarios and having more discussions with Dick revealed that some whole-part hierarchies were required. First, they focused on the other type of Rental Equipment, the Boat class.

At DDT some boats are rented with a trailer, some without a motor, and some with one or two motors. Trailers and motors always stay with the same boat; they are never rented by themselves or taken away from the boat they belong to (except to be serviced or replaced). This is the same situation that was described in Chapter 7, and we will use the same whole-part hierarchy here, in Figure 9.9.

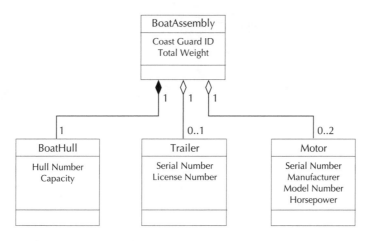

Figure 9.9   Boat assembly whole-part hierarchy

If all Dick needs to know about these things is if they are included or not, this can be indicated by using an attribute (such as a flag) for each of them in the Boat class. If we need more information, the Boat class is really a Boat Assembly class that includes a Boat Hull, Motor(s), and a Trailer.

In a whole-part hierarchy, the cardinality (multiplicity) of the relationships among the whole and its parts must be defined. Additionally, some relationships in the whole-part hierarchy might be optional (a boat assembly might not include a trailer or a motor), and some relationships might be mandatory (a boat assembly must include a boat hull).

Back when the consultants defined the Rental Equipment class and refined the Diving Equipment class, they made some notes about another important issue. Does a customer rent one piece of equipment, or does the customer rent many pieces of equipment? The consultants first thought about this issue when they realized that diving requires quite a few separate items. A customer is not likely to rent just a regulator or just a weight belt. But at the same time, it is not feasible to view diving equipment as a collection of items that are always rented as a package. Also, when they focused on the Customer class, they found that many customers rent both diving equipment and a boat. Therefore, some provision for allowing a contract to include many pieces of equipment is required.

They focused on the Contract class and decided that a Contract contains, or includes, many items of equipment, which they named the Contract Item class. Each Contract Item is "part of" one Contract, so they defined a whole-part hierarchy that contains a Contract and its Contract Items, as shown in Figure 9-10.

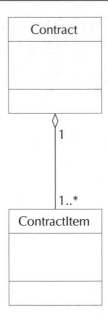

Figure 9.10   Contract whole-part hierarchy

The consultants again turned to the list of use cases and scenarios and confirmed that the whole-part hierarchies were consistent with the scenarios. The scenarios were brought up to date. For example, when *a customer rents equipment*, Contract is responsible for creating each Contract Item object, and Contract Item is in turn responsible for getting the rental price from each piece of Rental Equipment.

Identifying and Specifying Attributes

The consultants then began to focus on attributes of the classes in the class diagram. Some of the attributes were considered and noted when the generalization/specialization hierarchies and whole-part hierarchies were developed. Some object-oriented methods assume that specific attributes are not needed until physical design or implementation. However, for business information systems, a fairly good understanding of some of the important attributes is required during object-oriented analysis. The model need not be complete at this stage, and additional attributes can be added later.

The choice of which attributes to include is based on an understanding of how the objects are described in the problem domain, the responsibilities they will have in the information system, and what they need to know or remember.

For Customer, the consultants add attributes such as Name and Address, although the address might also be an appropriate attribute of Contract. It is sometimes difficult to decide where to place an attribute, so the consultants always go back to Dick with questions. The consultants chose to use Address as an attribute, rather than specifying Street, City, State, and Zip Code separately, to reduce the amount of detail put in the model at this stage.

The consultants had already identified attributes when they refined the generalization/specialization hierarchy for customers into whole-part relationships. Some attributes were also included for the Boat Assembly, Boat Hull, Trailer, Motor, and other classes. Figure 9.11 shows all of the classes in the object model with their important attributes. Naturally, the consultants reviewed the list of use cases and the scenarios and brought them up to date.

Identifying Additional Relationships

Figure 9.11 shows all of the classes, but not all of them are connected. Although classes in a class diagram might not be associated with other classes, there are associations that are probably required. So, the consultants began to look for association relationships that needed to be added.

The consultants identified several association relationships. For example, each Contract Item needs to be associated with the Rental Equipment that is rented. Each piece of Rental Equipment is rented many times, and over time it is associated with many Contract Item objects. A Contract item is associated, however, with one piece of Rental Equipment only. Therefore, the relationship is one to many between Rental Equipment and Contract Item and one to one between Contract Item and Rental Equipment.

There is also a relationship between Customer and Contract. Hopefully, each Customer will return and rent some equipment again and again. A Customer might be associated with many Contracts, but a Contract is related to one Customer only. The class diagram that includes these two relationships is shown in Figure 9.12.

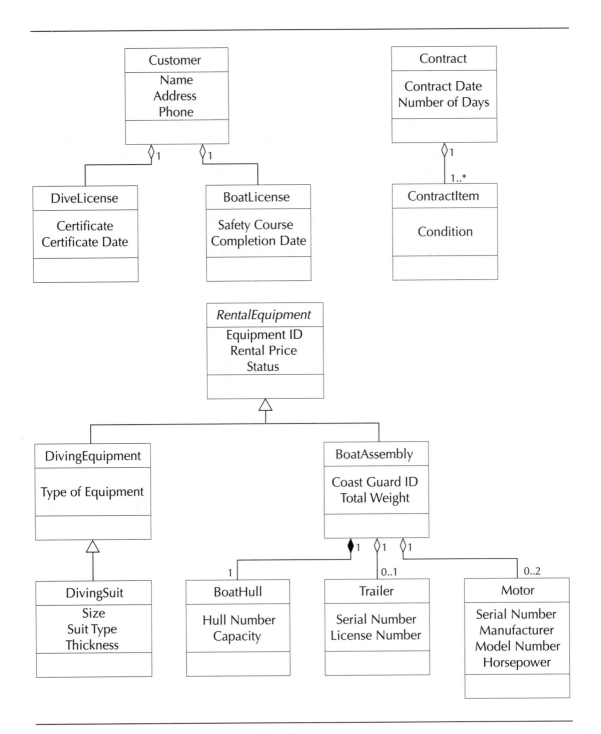

Figure 9.11 Class diagram showing initial attributes

Chapter 9

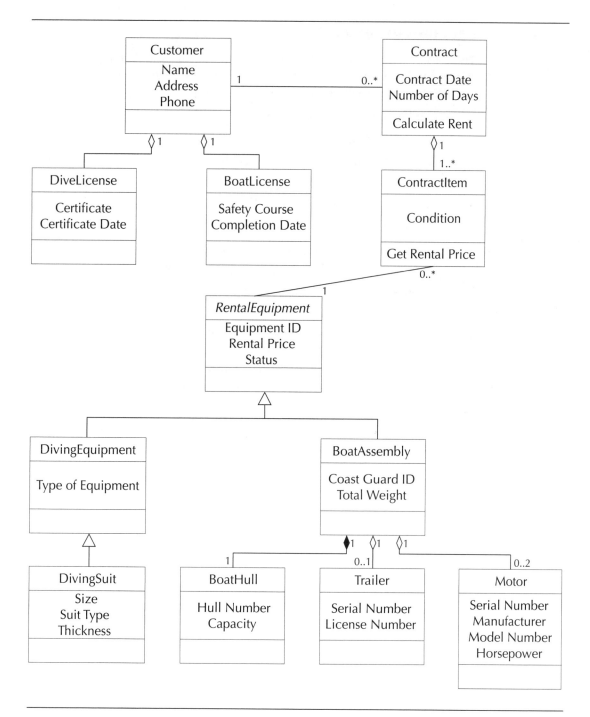

Figure 9.12   Class diagram showing association relationships and custom methods

Second-Cut Scenarios

The consultants needed to refine the four scenarios for the Rent equipment use case further once the classes had been expanded. The "rent boat equipment to an existing customer" scenario shown on the previous page was expanded as follows:

Event: Customer rents something

Use Case: Rent equipment

Scenario: Rent boat assembly to existing customer

> The user asks Contract to create a new Contract object for an existing customer, based on a customer ID.
>
> Contract connects to the correct Customer object.
>
> The Customer object asks its Boat License object for license details and returns all customer information to the Contract object.
>
> Contract asks Contract Item to create a new object and to connect to the Contract.
>
> Contract Item asks the user for the boat ID since it is a boat rental contract, which the user supplies.
>
> Contract Item connects to the correct Boat Assembly and gets boat details, including the amount to charge for the rental, which it returns to Contract.
>
> Contract provides contract details to the user in whatever form the user might require.

Notice that the expanded scenario follows the same general sequence as the initial scenario, and the responsibilities assigned to objects remain the same. Additional objects are involved because the number of classes involved in the scenario has expanded. A sequence diagram that documents the scenario is shown in Figure 9.13.

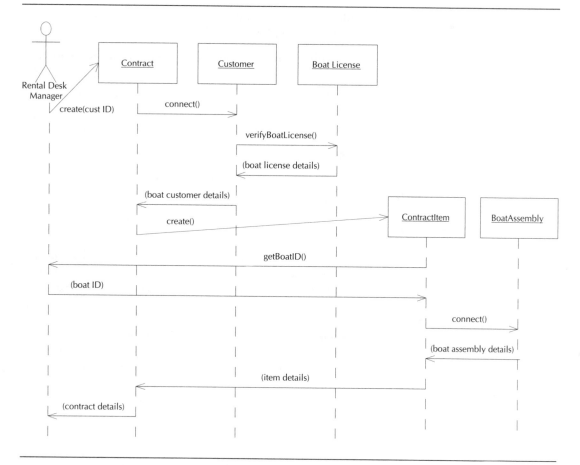

Figure 9.13   Refined Sequence diagram for scenario: Rent Boat Assembly to Existing Customer with a Boat License

The expanded scenario for "rent boat equipment to new customer" is also a variation on its initial scenario. It is shown below, and the sequence diagram that documents the scenario is shown in Figure 9.14:

Scenario: Rent boat assembly to new customer

The user asks Contract to create a new Contract object for a new customer.

Contract knows it needs to create a new Customer, so it asks Customer to create a new Customer object.

Customer needs information to create itself, so the new Customer object asks the user for name, address, and information about the boat license.

The user supplies the requested information, the Customer object creates a new Boat License object, and then supplies all customer details to Contract.

Contract asks Contract Item to create a new object and to connect to the Contract.

Contract Item asks the user for the boat ID since it is a boat rental contract, which the user supplies.

Contract Item connects to the correct Boat Assembly and gets boat details, including the amount to charge for the rental, which it returns to Contract.

Contract provides contract details to the user in whatever form the user might require.

Identifying Methods

As is evident in the scenarios above, the consultants decided earlier that the Contract class would be responsible for much of the processing when a customer rents something. This decision was reevaluated as the scenarios and the class diagram were reviewed. For example, Rental Equipment could be assigned the responsibility for the processing required when it "rents itself." The scenarios written for each use case would be quite different if the responsibilities were changed. Everything in the model should be challenged and reviewed during the development process. The consultants decided, however, that the Contract class was still the best choice, so they began to consider the methods that might be required.

Many of Contract's responsibilities require only standard methods, which are implicit in the class diagram. To fully carry out its responsibilities, though, Contract needs to calculate how much to charge for the rental. Calculating what to charge is not standard, so a custom method was required, which the consultants named Calculate Rent. The custom method name was added to the Contract class in the class diagram. The consultants then tried to figure out what Contract had to do to make the calculation. They expanded the scenario Rent equipment scenarios to explore the possibilities.

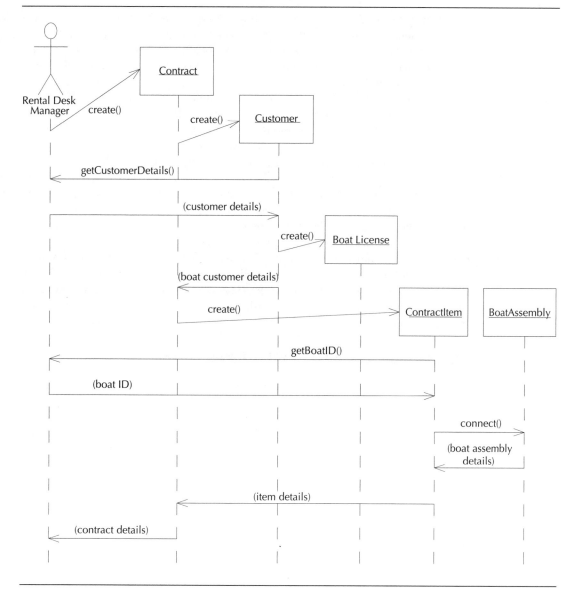

Figure 9.14   Refined Sequence diagram for scenario: Rent Boat Assembly to New Customer

They concluded that Contract needs to ask each Contract Item how much each piece of equipment costs to rent each day. Then Contract can sum up the individual values and come up with the total. They next took a closer look at Contract Item. For Contract Item to know what a piece of equipment costs, it needs to ask Rental Equipment. Rental Equipment knows what each piece of equipment costs to rent because the Rental Price is an attribute of the Rental Equipment class. Therefore, the consultants added a custom method to Contract Item, called Get Rental Price, but no custom method was required for Rental Equipment. These methods are included in the class diagram shown in Figure 9.12.

The scenario refinements made to define the custom methods needed in Contract and Contract Item also showed the need for interaction between Contract and Contract Item, and between Contract Item and Rental Equipment. The scenario also showed that Contract needs to send a message to Customer to ask for verification that the customer is qualified to rent the equipment (e.g., the Customer has a related Dive license, if diving equipment is rented). Additionally, Contract might need to ask Customer to "create itself" if it is a new customer. Finally, Contract needs to ask Contract Item to "create itself" for each piece of equipment rented.

The consultants supplemented the class diagram by writing descriptions of the custom methods. Structured English, pseudocode, action diagrams, or similar notations can be used for this process.

Identifying Time-Dependent Behavior

In Chapter 5, the statechart diagram was described as an additional graphical model used during object-oriented analysis when there are important rules governing the behavior of an object. An object might be in one of several states. Consider a Rental Equipment object. It can be available for rent, it can be rented (and thus unavailable), or it can be out of service (for repair or maintenance). All the objects in the class have the same potential states. The object can be thought of as having a life cycle, a sequence of states the object can go through in its lifetime. At some time the object is created, it then goes through various states, and finally it is deleted. What we model with the statechart is all the allowable sequences of states that can occur. Figure 9.15 shows an example for the Rental Equipment class. States are shown as boxes, and the transitions are shown as arrows.

The consultants focused on the Rental Equipment class because these objects go through a life cycle that is particularly important because one of the objectives of the system is better control of inventory. Customers go through a life cycle, too, as do all of the classes.

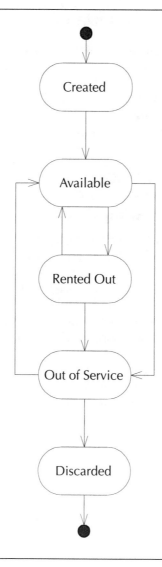

Figure 9.15   Statechart for state transitions of the Rental Equipment class

Moving on with the Development Process

The consultants wanted to develop the system iteratively and incrementally, as suggested by most development methods such as the Rational Unified Process (RUP). After they completed scenarios and sequence diagrams for the Rent equipment use case, they decided that the class diagram was complete enough for them to start designing the system and implementing the Rent equipment use case. They finalized the analysis documentation for this first iteration. Everything needed to be reviewed and double-checked, the documentation needed to be cleaned up and made presentable, and the users needed to walk through the use case and scenarios and verify that all relevant functionality was present.

Finalizing the Analysis Documentation

In parallel with the design and implementation of the first use case they started planning the work on the next iteration. Eventually the scenarios for all the use cases will have been accounted for and the analysis documentation completed and finalized.

Again, it is important to remember that the analysis phase does not end abruptly, and during design and implementation the scenarios, sequence diagrams, and class diagram will be added to and refined.

The consultants working for DDT finalized the class diagram and use case model, worked through each use case, completed the scenario descriptions and sequence diagrams, and created a model showing packages to use as an overview of the system. Based on the models presented by the consultants, Dick felt that the object-oriented analysis approach worked well. The consultants seemed to have a very clear understanding of the business and what Dick needed the system to do.

Review Questions

1. What are the four activities of object-oriented analysis?

2. Which of the activities are done in parallel?

3. What are some ways to initially identify classes?

4. What is the role of use cases and scenarios when building the requirements model?

5. What is the relationship between a written scenario and a sequence diagram?

6. What is the difference between the top-down approach and the bottom-up approach for identifying generalization/specialization hierarchies and whole-part hierarchies?

7. Explain why identifying a generalization/specialization hierarchy requires identifying some attributes of the classes.

8. Explain how scenarios and sequence diagrams are used to find messages and methods that are required.

9. What graphical model documents time-dependent behavior?

10. What are the reasons for clustering classes and defining packages?

Discussion Questions

1. In the DDT case, the consultants knew very little about the equipment rental business when they began. At the end of the case, Dick mentioned that they seemed to understand very well what the system needed to do. To what extent, then, is the analysis process a learning process for the analyst? Is the object-oriented approach a more natural approach for the analyst to use to learn something?

2. An iterative, incremental approach to development is assumed in the DDT case. An important use case might be implemented as a prototype before addressing the requirements of additional use cases. To what extent is the class diagram relatively complete after developing just one use case in the DDT case? Why would an important use case involve most or even all of the problem domain classes of the system?

3. After completing the Rent equipment use case, what is the next use case you would choose to work on if you were running this project? Why?

Exercises

1. Write descriptions for the two scenarios of the Rent equipment use case that were not shown in the text: "rent diving equipment to an existing dive customer" and "rent diving equipment to a new customer." Create sequence diagrams to document the scenarios.

2. Consider whether a separate scenario should be written for the situation in which an existing boat customer wants to rent dive equipment for the first time. Write a description for the scenario and create a sequence diagram.

3.   All objects go through a life cycle. Create a statechart for Customer encompassing each of the following: the customer is added, is in good standing, has equipment, is in default, and is deleted. Create a statechart for Contract.

4.   What if Dick rented different types of boats, such as trailerable boats, motor boats, and row boats, each with different parts? Revise the class diagram to show this.

5.   What if Dick had two different types of contracts, long-term rentals (leases) and short-term rentals. Revise the class diagram to show this.

6.   Write a description of the scenario "add new diving equipment." Create a sequence diagram to document the scenario.

7.   What are some additional scenarios that might be included for the Add new equipment use case to handle all of the special situations? For any one of the special situations, write a description of the scenario and create a sequence diagram.

Object-Oriented Design

10

Introduction

As discussed in Chapter 8, object-oriented development is a highly iterative process. It is difficult to define when object-oriented analysis ends and object-oriented design begins. It is equally difficult to define when object-oriented design ends and object-oriented implementation begins. One reason for this is the extensive use of prototyping, whereby the developer completes part of the requirements model, adds physical design details to the model, and then implements part of the system for testing and evaluation by end users.

The other reason why the analysis, design, and implementation phases are difficult to separate is that in object-oriented development, the UML diagrams and the scenarios produced during the analysis phase are refined and expanded during the design phase. Then, the same diagrams and scenarios are implemented on the computer during object-oriented implementation. The developers are always working with classes and objects, so it is difficult to look over their shoulders and observe what life cycle phase they are working on.

In this chapter, we describe some of the activities of the object-oriented design phase to highlight the issues that are addressed. After completing this chapter, you should understand some of the refinements and additions to the UML diagrams and the scenarios that occur during object-oriented design.

What Is Object-Oriented Design?

System design means completing a detailed specification of how a computer system will be implemented. The design specification is usually referred to as a physical model because it includes implementation details. The requirements models discussed in previous chapters are logical models of the system and are produced during the object-oriented analysis phase. A logical model specifies what is required without defining implementation details.

What is missing from the requirements models? In other words, what implementation details have to be added to the requirements model to make it a design model? First, although the classes of objects from the problem domain of the users have been defined during object-oriented analysis, there is no indication of how the classes of objects will be implemented on the computer. The standard and custom methods have to be written, validation and exception handling have to be defined, system controls must be designed, and database management functions have to be addressed. The approaches taken to these issues are usually determined by the programming language or development tools to be used.

Once a specific object-oriented language or development tool is selected, there are many additional unresolved questions. For example, what predefined classes or class libraries are available, and what predefined classes can be used?

What object-oriented features does the development tool support? For example, does it allow multiple inheritance? Does it support object persistence with relational databases, with object-oriented database management, or both?

Object-oriented design, then, requires developers to focus on the specific programming language and development tools that will be used to implement the system. Explaining how to design for a specific language and specific development tools is beyond the scope of this book, although the next chapter describes some object-oriented languages, some development tools, and some implementation issues.

But what else is missing from the requirements model that should be added during object-oriented design? Although the UML diagrams and scenarios in previous chapters included the actor (a user) interacting with problem domain objects, they did not indicate *how* the user interaction would be implemented. Therefore, the most obvious omission is the set of objects that make up the user interface of the system. In Chapter 2, we discussed user interface objects, such as windows, dialog boxes, pull-down menus, and buttons. These user interface objects can be added to the requirements model to show how the user will actually interact with the system. The UML diagrams and the scenario descriptions become much more detailed during object-oriented design as the user interface classes and objects are added.

Three-Tier Design Architecture

A **three-tier design architecture** based on the client-server model is usually used to organize the system design components into separate packages. The three design components discussed below represent broad areas that involve design activities, and they correspond to the three types of objects discussed in Chapter 2. These components are:

- The problem domain component
- The operating environment component
- The user interface component

The problem domain component is primarily addressed during analysis, but the operating environment and user interface components are added during design. Figure 10.1 shows the three components in a UML package diagram. Each package contains classes that make up the design component.

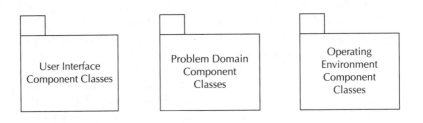

Figure 10.1   Components in the three-tier design architecture as a Package diagram

The **problem domain component** is the model of the classes of objects that are part of the work environment of the users, begun during the analysis phase. The focus changes from modeling the requirements independent of technology to modeling a system that can be implemented with specific technology. During object-oriented design, the model is refined and possibly expanded as the analyst continues to uncover and understand more about the user's requirements for the system and the implementation implications.

There needs to be some refinement of the class diagram. Addressing contingency scenarios, error handling, and so on will likely reveal more classes and more attributes of existing classes. Many-to-many relationships need to be investigated and possibly changed. Specifications of attributes have to be finalized and defined in detail. Standard methods have to be written, and custom methods need to be specified to a greater level of detail. There needs to be a critical evaluation of classes and hierarchies to identify and correct potential processing problems that result from overspecialization or unsuitable subclasses.

Other refinements made to the problem domain component have to do with changes required by the development environment. For example, C++ allows multiple inheritance, but Java and Smalltalk do not. Therefore, a class diagram that contains multiple inheritance might have to be reworked due to constraints of a programming language.

The **operating environment component** defines the system's interaction with operating systems, printers, network devices, database management systems, or other information systems. The issues that arise are highly dependent on the available technology. Many system controls added during the design phase involve the operating environment.

By separating the operating environment component from the problem domain component, the design will be more flexible when handling later changes in the technological environment. Later changes in operating systems, networks, database management systems, and other information systems are likely to affect only the operating environment.

The **user interface component** defines how the user will interact with the computer system. The user interface component is obviously very important to the users. Additionally, user interface design concepts and techniques are generally applicable no matter what development environment is used, so we will emphasize this component more than others in this chapter.

Figure 10.2 shows a sequence diagram that demonstrates generically how the three components interact in a scenario. First, the actor interacts with user interface objects assembled on a window—a graphical user interface (GUI). The actor sends messages to the GUI by choosing menu items, pushing buttons, selecting items in lists, and typing into text boxes. The GUI in turn sends messages to problem domain objects based on the messages it gets from the actor. The interface objects making up the GUI are therefore placed between the actor and the problem domain objects during design. The problem domain objects send necessary messages to operating environment objects, such as network devices and databases.

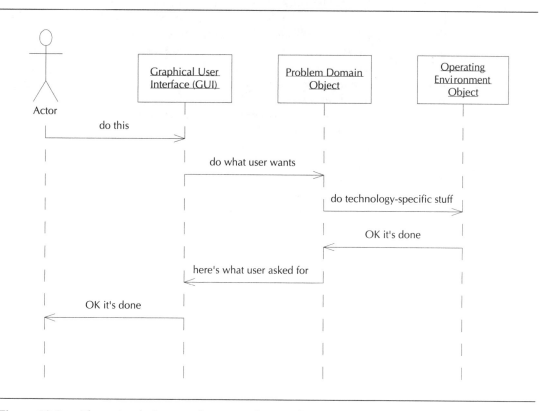

Figure 10.2   Three-tier design as a Sequence diagram for a generic scenario

Designing for the Operating Environment

One of the most important parts of the operating environment for an information system is the database management system that stores information created and used by the system. In an object-oriented system, the database management system must manage the data that describe the problem domain objects in the system, such as customers, products, orders, and shipments. Once an object is created, it must be stored and later retrieved on demand. Such objects are called **persistent objects** because they must be available over time. Various approaches to database management for persistent objects are discussed in Chapter 11.

No matter which approach to database management is used, the three-tier design approach defines a separate data manager class for each persistent problem domain class. The details of storing and retrieving data are the responsibilities of the data manager class. The problem domain class is given methods for storing and restoring data, but they only involve asking the corresponding data manager class to do the work. The data manager class is designed to store and restore data based on the database management system used. Therefore, when the data manager class is asked to store information about an object, its "store" method might be designed to use SQL to update tables in a relational database or it might be designed to store the object directly in an object-oriented database. Keeping the database access separate from the problem domain classes makes the system more flexible and easier to maintain and enhance.

Figure 10.3 shows a sequence diagram for the scenario "add new video" for the video collector system from Chapter 6. The user interface component is represented by a Video Item GUI. The actor interacts with the GUI to provide information about the new video, and then the GUI interacts with the Video Item problem domain object. The Video Item object interacts with the Video Item data manager class to establish a record of the new Video object in the database.

Another important aspect of the operating environment is integrating with existing system components or legacy systems. A **component** is a software module that is fully assembled and ready to use. It might be a collection of objects or it might be a non-OO program that has been "wrapped" to behave like an object. In order to facilitate the use of interchangeable components, standards are used to define methods for connecting them. The decision to use one of the standards affects system design and the choice of languages and development tools. Two standards are well developed and widely used. The **Common Object Request Broker Architecture (CORBA)** is backed by the Object Management Group (OMG), a consortium of software and hardware vendors. The **Distributed Component Object Model (DCOM)** is backed by Microsoft.

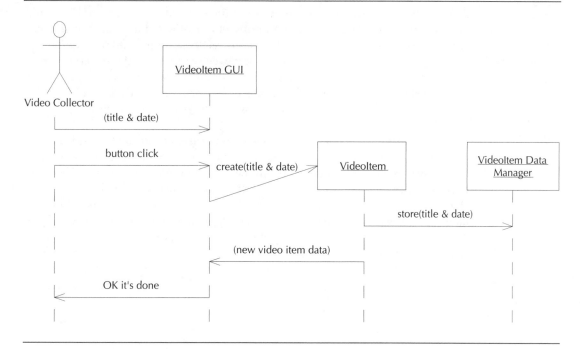

Figure 10.3   Three-tier design for scenario: Add New Video Item

Designing the User Interface

The user interface of a computer system is usually thought of as the physical devices through which a user interacts with a computer, such as a keyboard or mouse, and the objects that the user sees on the computer screen. Most information systems developers are interested in graphical user interfaces (GUI), and these interfaces usually allow direct manipulation of objects on the screen. For example, the user clicks a button on the screen or drags an object from one place to another on the screen. As we discussed in Chapter 2, to many system developers, object-oriented development means graphical user interfaces.

To the user, the user interface is the system itself, so in the broadest sense, everything the user comes into contact with while using the system is part of the user interface. In a direct manipulation system, the user comes into contact with graphical representations of objects from the problem domain, so it is difficult for the user to separate the user interface objects from the problem domain objects defined during systems analysis. Class names, attribute names, relationship names, and method names selected during object-oriented analysis become part of the interface to the users because the users see these names and phrases in messages, in menus, and in labels. They might even see icons on the screen that represent problem domain objects (a patient, a video, a boat). Therefore, part of the user interface begins to emerge during object-oriented analysis, and the user interface that is designed is based on some of the decisions made during object-oriented analysis.

The user interface objects and the communication protocols are added to the requirements model and scenarios during object-oriented design. The user interface objects required in the system can be shown on a class diagram. There are fairly standard generalization/specialization hierarchies and whole-part hierarchies of interface objects. For example, Figure 10-4 shows the class of objects named Menu with two specialized classes: Pop-Up Menu and Pull-Down Menu. These two types of menus are quite common in graphical user interfaces. Examples are shown in Figure 10.5.

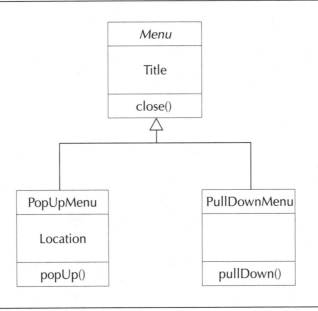

Figure 10.4   Generalization/specialization hierarchy for Menu classes

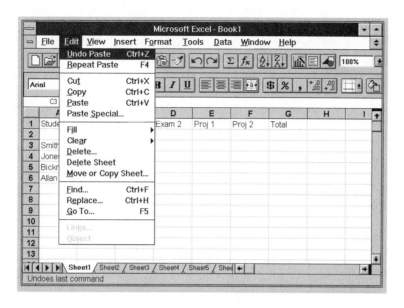

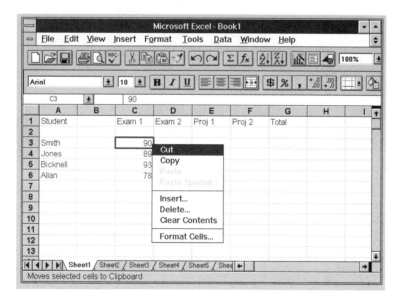

Figure 10.5   Pull-down and pop-up menu examples

The whole-part hierarchy is also quite applicable to user interface objects. A menu bar "contains" pull-down menus and each pull-down menu "contains" menu items, as shown in Figure 10.6. The overall structure of the graphical user interface usually involves windows, and since a window can contain many different types of interface objects, the whole-part hierarchy is also useful for showing a window and its parts (Figure 10.7). Predefined classes of user interface objects are readily available in class libraries that come with languages and development environments, so these classes do not have to be designed from scratch for each new system.

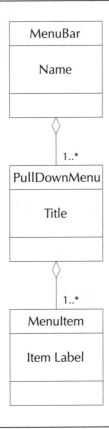

Figure 10.6   Whole-part hierarchy (aggregation) of MenuBar containing PullDownMenus with MenuItems

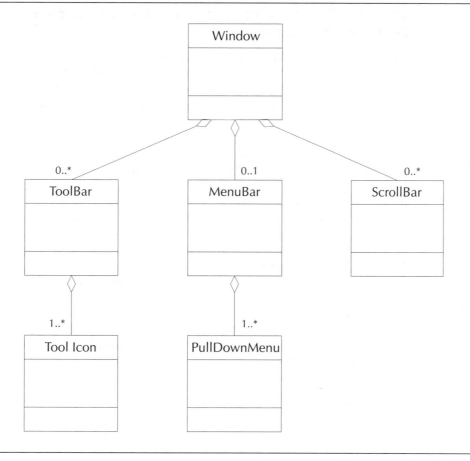

Figure 10.7   Whole-part hierarchy (aggregation) of a Window and its parts

Using a class diagram to define the user interface objects that will be used in the system results in several benefits. First, the interface objects are defined using the same diagramming conventions as the requirements model. Using a class diagram will also get the designer thinking more in terms of a variety of interface objects, so it is more likely that the most usable object will be selected for each design decision. Finally, and of great importance, creating a class diagram will help ensure that the interface objects are defined and used consistently, resulting in a consistent user interface. User interface consistency has been notoriously difficult to achieve, and inconsistent interfaces cause great frustration for users (as well as being costly in terms of training and user errors).

Interface Design Enhancements to Scenarios and Sequence Diagrams

User interface objects can be added to written scenarios and sequence diagrams to expand the detail shown about a scenario. The example in Figure 10.3 shows the user interface as one GUI object, but the GUI object is actually a collection of interface objects, including menus, buttons, text boxes, lists, and even dialog boxes. A written scenario can be used to explore the details of the interaction the user has with the GUI.

The written scenarios from the analysis phase can be expanded to specify the user interface design by adding references to the user interface objects in the scenario description. As with the class diagram, the written scenarios are added to during object-oriented design. Again, models created during analysis are expanded; nothing is thrown away. Again, the same notation used during analysis is used during design.

User interface design is often called dialog design, because the interface allows the user and the computer to communicate, often in the form of a dialog. The scenarios shown in Chapters 6 and 7 were written like a dialog. For example, the user requests that a class of objects add a new object, and the class of objects responds with a request for information. Then the user supplies the requested information.

The designer can take these dialogs and add more specific interface design details. For example, the scenario for "add new video" can be enhanced by including the interface objects shown in bold:

Event: You get a new video.
Use Case: Add new video, main scenario

The user clicks the **Add Video Menu Item** on the **VideoItem Window**

The **VideoItem Window** knows that it needs the Title and Date Acquired, so it displays the **Add VideoItem Dialog Box**, which contains **Text Boxes** for Title and Date Acquired, with a **Prompt** stating "Please enter the Title and Date Acquired for the new Video Item."

The user types the Title and Date Acquired values in the **Text Boxes**, and clicks the **"OK" Command Button** contained in the dialog box.

The **Add VideoItem Dialog Box** returns the Title and Date Acquired to the **VideoItem Window**.

The **VideoItem Window** asks VideoItem to create a new VideoItem using the title and date acquired.

A sequence diagram can also be used to show the additional details of the interface design based on the written scenario, as shown in Figure 10.8. A class diagram can be drawn to show all of the interface objects involved in the scenario as well, as shown in Figure 10.9.

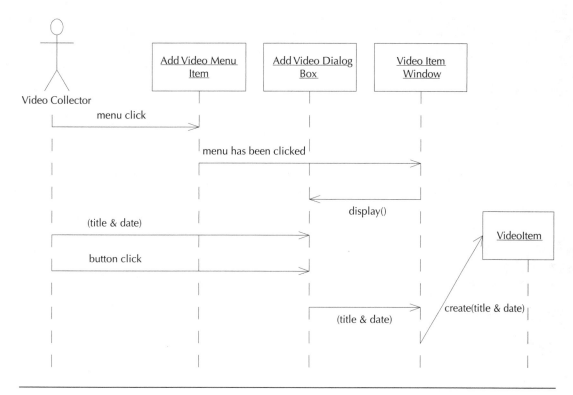

Figure 10.8   Interface design details for scenario: Add New Video Item

The Interface and the Overall System Structure

Another important system design activity is the design of the overall system structure, which can be represented by the design of the system menus and the navigation paths. Menu items are selected by the user to tell objects in the system what to do. The menu item names and some hierarchical organization of the menu items must be defined. An example of a generic word-processor menu hierarchy is shown in Figure 10.10. Menu names at the top level include File, Edit, Format, and Help. Under each of these menus is a list of menu items. This is an example of a two-level menu structure, organized around the types of operations a user might request of a document object.

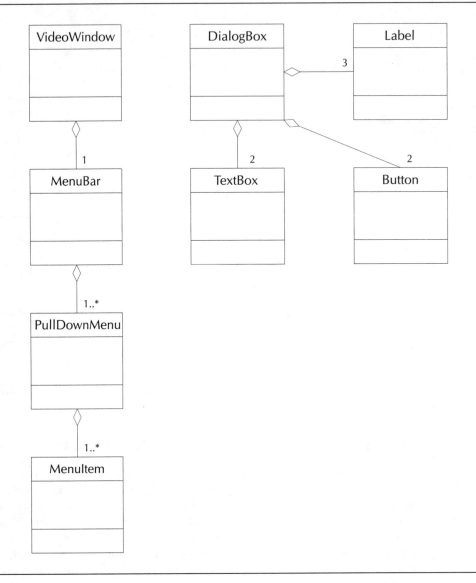

Figure 10.9   Class diagram showing Interface classes used in the "Add New Video Item" scenario

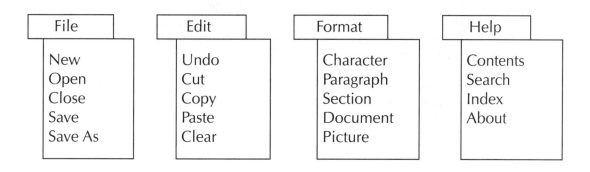

Figure 10.10　Generic word-processor menu hierarchies

Information systems, such as order entry, inventory management, or employee benefits, also typically use menus, and these are the types of systems developed by information systems staff. Most of the object-oriented design examples found in design and programming books are based on document objects, and the pattern of File, Edit, and Format for the menus does not usually apply to information systems.

Where might the designer look to find what should appear in the menus? The menu items required in the system will correspond closely to the list of events that lead to use cases and scenarios, so the scenarios written during object-oriented analysis provide the key. In the example of the more complete system required by a video collector (in Chapter 6), there were five events, and five corresponding use cases and main scenarios involving two classes of objects:

1.　Event: Collector gets a new video.
　　Use Case: Add new video, main scenario

2.　Event: Collector wants to see a list of videos.
　　Use case: Look up video information, main scenario

3.　Event: Collector wants to correct information about a video.
　　Use Case: Update video information, main scenario

4.　Event: Collector loses or damages a video.
　　Use Case: Delete video, main scenario

5.　Event: Collector views a video.
　　Use case: Record viewing, main scenario

The menu hierarchy shown in Figure 10.11 provides the user with the ability to start the interactions described in the five main scenarios (the event number is in parentheses). There are three important design decisions reflected in this menu hierarchy. First, the request for video information (number 2) has been refined to show three possible information queries that the user needs. Each of these is an example of an additional scenario for the use case—search for a video, list video titles, and list recently viewed videos. These specific queries were added during design. During analysis, the query capability was assumed to allow any number of specific requests, but the details were not yet specified. The second design decision is to include three scenarios or use cases under one higher-level menu item, named inventory management (numbers 1, 3, and 4). Finally, a help system has been included, under the Help menu item.

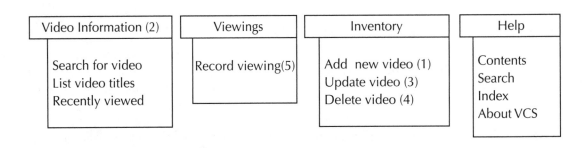

Figure 10.11   Initial Video Collector system menu design

The menu hierarchy design can also be coordinated with the Operating Environment component. Figure 10.12 shows an additional menu hierarchy that includes user preference settings, backup and recovery, user accounts, and access to system utilities, such as those used for configuring printers and other devices.

Another issue to consider in the design of the menu hierarchy is the variety of users that might interact with the system. One menu design might fit the work of one set of users, but another design might be better for other users. Additionally, several alternative designs might be proposed. Therefore, prototyping and evaluation by users will help identify the most effective design of the overall system structure and user interface. The users should be very involved in the design process.

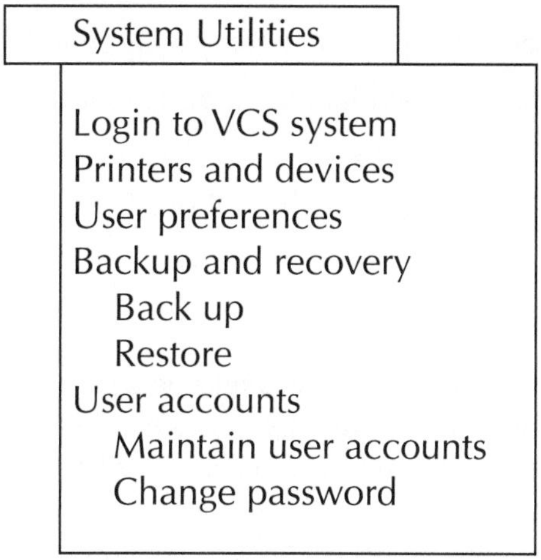

```
┌─────────────────────────────┐
│  System Utilities           │
├─────────────────────────────┴──┐
│                                 │
│  Login to VCS system            │
│  Printers and devices           │
│  User preferences               │
│  Backup and recovery            │
│      Back up                    │
│      Restore                    │
│  User accounts                  │
│      Maintain user accounts     │
│      Change password            │
│                                 │
│                                 │
└─────────────────────────────────┘
```

Figure 10.12   Additional menu added to Video Collector system for user preferences and system controls

■ Key Terms

Common Object Request
  Broker Architecture
  (CORBA)
component
Distributed Component
  Object Model (DCOM)

operating environment
  component
persistent objects
problem domain
  component

system design
three-tier design architecture
user interface component

■ Review Questions

1. What are the reasons that it is difficult to define when analysis ends and design begins?

2. What are some of the "technical" issues that must be considered during design?

3. What is added to the UML diagrams and the scenario descriptions that make these models more physical during design?

4. What are the three main design components?

5. What does the operating environment component define?

6. What does the user interface component define?

7. Why does a class diagram of the user interface help ensure a consistent user interface?

8. Why is the menu hierarchy one way to define the overall system structure?

■ Discussion Question

1. In object-oriented analysis and design, the same models and notations are used in both phases, but more details are added to the model during the design phase. How does this help ensure that the requirements defined during analysis are not overlooked during design, as compared to the transition from structured analysis to structured design?

■ Exercises

1. An exercise in Chapter 9 required writing a scenario description and drawing a sequence diagram for adding a new piece of rental equipment. Enhance the solution to show user interaction with interface objects such as selection lists, check boxes, and radio buttons.

2. Create a menu hierarchy for the complete system required by Dick's Dive 'n' Thrive from Chapter 9. Now try to create some alternate designs that might work just as well. Prototype the alternatives with Visual Basic or a similar tool. Then, ask some friends to evaluate the menu designs and give you their preferences. Is there only one best design?

Object-Oriented Development Tools

11

Introduction

This book emphasizes object-oriented thinking, object-oriented concepts, object-oriented requirements models, and the object-oriented analysis process. Object-oriented design is discussed only generally. One reason for this is that the main object-oriented concepts and the object-oriented approach can be understood in the context of the systems analysis models and methods. The other reason for the requirements model and analysis process emphasis is that with detailed design and implementation, very technical issues must be addressed. The specifics depend upon the development environment used for the system, so such details will not be covered here.

This chapter describes some implementation tools and issues, including object-oriented programming languages, object-oriented database management, CASE tools for object-oriented development, and integrated development environments (IDE). When you complete this chapter, you should understand the types of tools that are available and some of the issues that might arise.

Object-Oriented Programming Languages

Object-oriented programming languages (OOPL) have existed since the early sixties. There are many object-oriented programming languages in existence today, probably close to a hundred, although most of these are research products not commercially available.

There are languages that support objects but not classes or inheritance. These are not usually considered object-oriented programming languages, but rather object-based languages. Ada and earlier versions of Visual Basic are the most prominent example of this group. Object-oriented programming languages support the main object-oriented concepts, such as objects and classes, message sending, inheritance, encapsulation, and polymorphism. There are two main types of object-oriented languages: pure object-oriented languages and hybrid languages.

Pure object-oriented languages were designed to support object-oriented concepts from the outset. These languages support the object-oriented approach in the sense that everything is considered an object belonging to a class. Smalltalk and Java are the best known examples of this group.

The hybrid languages are extensions of other, mainly procedural languages. They support the object-oriented approach, but do not require it. With hybrid languages, it is still possible to define functions, global variables, or procedures that are not encapsulated in objects, or do not belong to a class. The best known example of this group is C++, which is based on the C programming language. There are also object-oriented versions of COBOL.

Of the current commercially available languages, Java seems to be the most influential one. Microsoft has, however, just released an object-oriented version of Visual Basic as part of their Visual Studio development suite. This might well gain a large following for information system development.

Java

Java was released by Sun Microsystems in 1995. It was designed specifically to support development of Internet-based distributed systems. A lot of the system development effort in the IS field is directed toward this type of system. Java was designed to have the "look and feel" of the C++ language, but it enforces a completely object-oriented view of programming. It is simpler to learn and use than C++, but it is still a language that requires a considerable effort to master. It can be used to create complete applications that may run on a single computer or be distributed among servers and clients in a network. It can also be used to build small application modules, or applets, for use as part of a Web page.

Java programs are portable. They are compiled into Java bytecode that can be run anywhere in a network, on a server or client that has a Java virtual machine. Individual computer platform differences, such as instruction lengths, are recognized and accommodated locally just as the program is being executed. Platform-specific versions of the programs are no longer needed. Both of the major Web browsers include a Java virtual machine, and almost all major operating system developers (IBM, Microsoft, and others) have added Java compilers as part of their product offerings.

Visual Basic

As part of their development suite, Visual Studio.Net, Microsoft has released a new version of **Visual Basic** with additional object-oriented features that simplify the development of enterprise Web applications.

The most requested feature for Visual Basic has been support for implementation of inheritance, which is now included. The new version of Visual Basic also supports overloading and polymorphism, which allows Visual Basic to process objects differently, depending on their data type or class. Additionally, it provides the ability to redefine methods for derived classes.

A lot of people are familiar with Visual Basic. It has been used extensively for GUI development, and it has been known as a very user-friendly language. The new object-oriented version will provide the features needed for efficient serverside development, but retain the simplicity that has made earlier versions so popular. It is very likely that the object-oriented version will become a key language for object-oriented information system development and increase further the importance and prevalence of object orientation.

The C# Language

As part of the Visual Studio, Microsoft also recently introduced a new object-oriented language, **C#** ("C sharp"), a modern, object-oriented programming language built from the ground up to exploit the power of XML-based Web services on the .Net platform. With its Visual C++ development system heritage, C# will enable C and C++ developers to use existing skills to rapidly build sophisticated XML-based .Net applications.

The C++ Language

C++ is especially popular with programmers who develop software products or complex technical applications. Because it is a direct extension of the C language, learning the syntax of C++ is easy for a trained C programmer. The difference between the languages is small, with maybe as much as 80 to 90 percent of C++ remaining pure C. C programmers tend to view C++ as enhanced C, or C with additional features. It is thus natural for C programmers to embrace C++.

C++ is a compiled language. This is an advantage at run time because it allows efficient execution of the program. In development situations, however, it can slow the process down, because changes made to parts of the program require recompilation of the whole before the changes can be tested. Some other features (strong typing, early binding) also emphasize efficiency during execution more than efficiency during development. For complex systems that put a heavy demand on processing capacity, this is an important trade-off to consider.

C++ might allow a gradual transition to the object-oriented approach. It can be integrated with existing C programs, allowing organizations to utilize and build on existing applications. C++ is available from a number of vendors and for most operating systems. Most C++ vendors offer a class browser of some kind. There are also many third-party developers of class libraries for a wide range of applications. Classes for user interface development are available, but typical information systems class libraries (containing problem domain classes) are still scarce.

The Smalltalk Language

Smalltalk is a pure object-oriented language developed at Xerox PARC in the seventies. The syntax is fairly easy to learn, being much less complicated than Java and C++. Since it enforces object-oriented programming, it serves well as a vehicle for adopting object-oriented thinking. It is an interpreted language, allowing the developer to make changes and then test them out immediately. This facilitates a prototyping approach to development. The interpreter and other features can, however, cause run time performance to suffer, and the language might not be suitable for complex processing and time-critical systems.

Object-Oriented COBOL

The Codasyl COBOL committee has defined standards for an object-oriented version of COBOL. The newest ANSI/ISO COBOL standard, which is scheduled to come into effect by 2002, will include provisions for OO programming and all the important OO concepts. The object-oriented version is meant to be compatible with standard COBOL, allowing existing applications to work with applications developed with the new technology. Although the standard has not yet come into effect, many vendors offer object-oriented extensions of their COBOL compilers, and Merant/Microfocus, Hitachi, Fujitsu, and IBM all have object-oriented COBOL products available.

COBOL is the foundation of a very large portion of business-related systems. The Web based e-commerce systems of today depend heavily on the COBOL-based legacy systems of the past. OO COBOL with its integration capabilities is thus likely to be an important factor in future business system development.

▌ Selecting a Language for Object-Oriented Information System Development

There are two sets of criteria that should be considered carefully before selecting one of the object-oriented programming languages. These are technical and commercial considerations. On the technical side, one should consider which language best supports the object-oriented concepts. The fit with existing hardware, software, and the skills of the employees is also important. On the commercial side, market penetration of the product is important. This will influence the availability of support and third-party products, such as class libraries, development environments, integration facilities, etc. Modern system development does not start from scratch and you choose a programming environment with integrated class libraries and other support tools more than you choose a language only.

Java is now the language of choice for many people, and the importance of Web-centric IS applications will likely only reinforce this. Java's prominence also ensures that a lot of new Java-oriented development will take place, so that there will be an increasing supply of class libraries, various support tools, and other third-party products available.

Object-oriented Visual Basic will, however, be a strong contender for the main language used for object-oriented information system development, partially because of its simplicity and the popularity of previous versions and partially because of Microsoft's general market penetration. The latter will ensure an abundance of third-party support tools and further enhancements of a Visual Basic programming environment with class libraries, testing and debugging facilities, etc.

C++ was for a while the preferred language for the more technical types of computer applications (avionics, device control, and other real-time applications). In these areas it allowed a gradual transition from C-based programming to C++.

Object-oriented COBOL might become an important language because it could revitalize and tie in with the vast number of COBOL applications in the information systems field. Moving to an object-oriented approach through object COBOL should also ease the transition for the large number of COBOL programmers in this field. This could by itself be an important consideration.

■ Object-Oriented Database Management

In object-oriented programming, the objects exist only during the program run. When the program is turned off, the objects are no longer available. They are, in essence, discarded. In information systems, we definitely need objects that are longer lived than that. When we get a new customer and create a related customer object, the customer information will be important to, and used by, the business for a long time.

Objects lasting beyond the program run are called **persistent objects**. The capability to handle persistent objects is one of the key technological issues to be considered by anyone contemplating an object-oriented approach to system development.

In all types of information systems, we usually need to store our data over a long period of time. We need those data to be current, available, and protected from unauthorized use. The main mechanism for achieving this is the database management system, or DBMS.

DBMSs have been used since the early seventies. The early systems were based on an underlying hierarchical data model. The next generation used a network model. Today, the main type of DBMS is based on the relational model.

Two different types of language features are used to manage the data in the database. The data definition language, or DDL, is used to specify the structure of the data (the database schema). The data manipulation language, or DML, is used to select and display the actual desired data.

In the relational DBMS, the data are stored as tables or relations. Relational technology is based on an extensive formal theory. The structured query language (SQL) has emerged as a de facto DML standard in the relational world. (Although SQL has several DDL features, other approaches to data definition are also used by the various DBMSs.)

Problems with Relational Databases

SQL operates with sets of data, a collection of rows in a table. A Select statement might give us a list of all the employees over 50 years of age. Standard programming languages, such as COBOL, can also be used to manipulate the data in the database.

Such languages usually handle one record at a time, and do not have any provisions to handle sets. There is thus a discrepancy between the ways the programming languages and the DBMS operate. This discrepancy is often referred to as the data impedance problem.

To obtain the desired view of data, different tables might have to be joined. This is a relatively time-consuming operation, and with large tables the performance might suffer severely. If we are able to handle persistent objects directly, the impedance problem is no longer relevant, because the unit we will be dealing with both in the database and in the application program is the object. The performance problem for complex views will also be solved. There will no longer be time-consuming joins involved because the object will be stored as a unit.

Handling Persistent Objects

There are three main approaches for handling persistent objects:

1. The relational approach
2. The extended relational approach
3. The (pure) object-oriented approach

No matter which approach is chosen, the system must, in addition to handling persistent objects, meet the same requirements for security, backup, recovery, and integrity that we expect from traditional DBMSs.

The Relational Approach to Persistent Objects

The data portion of the object might be transferred to tables in a standard relational DBMS. Method procedures might also be stored in other tables. When the object is needed, it would have to be reconstructed again from the tables.

Although possible, such an approach is cumbersome and will certainly lead to poor performance in larger systems. This approach allows us, however, to keep all code in existing DBMS intact. We can keep on using a type of product that is well known and stable. The considerable investment made to learn the relational DBMS could still provide a return.

Data from existing databases can also easily be transferred to the object-oriented application. In information systems this is a major concern, since new object-oriented systems are likely to deal with data that already exist in some other system. In systems where response time and database performance are not major concerns, this might be a viable solution, allowing us to reap the benefits of object-oriented applications while at the same time keeping the well proven and stable DBMS technology.

Object-Oriented Extensions to Relational Databases

This approach adds object-oriented functionality to relational DBMS, allowing the application programmer to store persistent objects without having to deal with relational conversions. The conversions that necessarily must take place are hidden from the user and handled by the system.

This approach also allows for easy integration with existing systems. Products are based on existing and well-known technology. And the major players in the relational DBMS arena, such as Oracle, Sybase, and Ingres, are all providing such extensions. Because of their position in the traditional information systems field, they are among the driving forces behind a gradual adoption of the object-oriented approach in mainstream information systems applications.

Object-Oriented Databases

There are commercial database systems available designed specifically to handle persistent objects. They provide an object-oriented storage mechanism combined with a direct interface to an object-oriented programming language. Some of them can be viewed as extensions to C++ or Java where those languages are used both as the DDL and the DML. Some have their own proprietary DDL, while a standard programming language is used as the DML. In addition to the programming language interface, most of them also provide some sort of high-level query language, either as an object-oriented version of SQL or through some proprietary query language.

The vendor companies of object-oriented databases are generally small and recently established. The first object-oriented database products were released in the late eighties. The products are still evolving, and the field is still not considered mature.

Object-oriented databases enable storage of complex data objects, such as video, sound, and images, that cannot conveniently or effectively be handled by traditional technology. It is within application areas requiring storage of such complex data objects that the object-oriented DBMSs have mainly been used.

Some of the available products in this group include:

Object Store from Excelon Corporation
Objectivity from Objectivity, Inc.
Versant Object Database Management System from Versant Corporation

Selecting a DBMS for Object-Oriented Information System Development

One major decision is whether to go with a hybrid or pure OODBMS approach. The need to interact with existing systems will often be a main consideration when selecting a database tool for modern Web-centric IS systems. This is one of the reasons why pure OODBMS have not become more prevalent in IS, and most IS development is done using the hybrid or OO extended relational type of tool.

Beyond this basic decision, two main types of considerations are those related to technical feasibility and market standing. The market situation is important for further development of the tool. The choice of a DBMS is usually a decision with long-term implications, and it is important that the vendor be capable of supporting and developing the tool in the future. From a recruiting point of view, it could also be easier to find and train people if one goes with one of the better-known products in the marketplace.

On the technological side, the tool will of course have to provide the functionality that is needed for the type of systems that are going to be built, and be compatible with other tools that are being used. The ability to integrate with existing applications and databases is often a major concern.

Some newer Integrated Development Environments (IDEs), such as Jasmine *ii* from Computer Associates, provide an integrated OODBMS and at the same time provide for integration with all the major relational DBMSs.

CASE Tools for Object-Oriented Development

CASE is an acronym for Computer-Aided Software (or Systems) Engineering. CASE tools are computer applications that provide support for system developers. Lower CASE tools support the later phases of systems development, such as code generating, debugging, and testing. Upper CASE tools provide support for the early, or upper, phases in the development life cycle, especially for the main modeling techniques being used. Although upper CASE functionality increased over the years, supporting many more aspects of analysis and design than only the main modeling techniques, it also became apparent that without integration with lower CASE tools, the benefits were fairly limited. This was the background for a new type of tool called Integrated CASE or **ICASE**. ICASE provides tools and method support for the whole development life cycle, from planning all the way through to implementation and maintenance.

The large ICASE tools have, however, not lived up to expectations and are partially discounted as yet another "silver bullet" solution that did not work. The problems with these tools were partially related to the learning curve when trying to use the actual tool. They often tended to be overly complex. Another set of problems was related to users having to learn and adapt to the new processes and approaches to system development that the tools enforced.

Presently, there are a lot of object-oriented lower CASE tools available that are important in the implementation phase. Object-oriented programming facilities have been around for a number of years, and are becoming quite sophisticated. Upper CASE tools are also available. There are a number of upper CASE tools that support UML. Some are quite comprehensive, while others are not much more than special-purpose drawing tools.

Comprehensive OOICASE tools, which have at least some of the ICASE features, are also available. Such tools support modeling and enable automated generation of code directly from the models. One of the most prominent examples of this type of tool is the Rational Suite (which includes Rational Rose) from Rational Software Corporation; another is Together 4 from TogetherSoft. Although fitting the definition of CASE tools, a lot of the tools available are not referred to as CASE tools by their vendors, mainly because the term has somewhat fallen from favor.

Selecting Object-Oriented ICASE Tools

At a minimum, the CASE tool must support the main modeling techniques being prescribed, which will almost certainly be UML. Models should be easy to make and change. Code generation capabilities are important. Without such capabilities, the tools remain little more than model-drawing tools. Ideally, tools should generate 100% complete code. There are a number of tools today that generate code to a smaller or larger extent. Most of these generate Java or C++ code. Either all maintenance and changes should be carried out on the specifications level and not on the actual code, or the tool should automatically update models and specifications if changes are made to the code. This is referred to as **round trip engineering**. If changes are done manually, specifications and actual code are bound to drift apart unless strict practices are followed.

Object-orientation enables alternative approaches to system development, such as prototype-driven incremental and iterative development, and the tool should support such alternative approaches. The more sophisticated tools will have process modeling and enactment facilities to allow users to tailor the development process to their individual projects.

One particularly important functionality needed in object-oriented CASE tools is support for finding reusable classes. This is of paramount importance for exploiting the reuse capability of the object-oriented approach. Extensive reuse of existing classes is the main productivity-enhancing feature of object-oriented development. As class libraries grow bigger, the potential for reuse increases, but so do the difficulties associated with finding the potential candidates for reuse.

Without support for this activity in the form of powerful class library browsers, extensive reuse will probably not occur.

Otherwise, there must be a repository to store all relevant project information. There must be a standard graphical user interface. There must be powerful cross-referencing, error-checking, and reporting facilities. There must be support for the tasks and techniques that the method prescribes, both for individual life cycle tasks, and for overall project tasks such as quality assurance, requirements tracing, version control, and project management. Standardization is necessary to allow different tools to communicate.

The extent of the functionality will of course vary widely between different tools, as will prices. The more powerful tools can greatly influence the approach to development and the process to follow and thus also the skills needed. Careful selection to ensure that the tool matches the tasks at hand and the capability of the organization is necessary.

◼ Integrated Development Environments (IDE)

Integrated development environment, or **IDE**, is a relatively new type of tool in the OO field. IDEs provide some of the functionality that is often associated with CASE tools. But in contrast to CASE tools, which usually existed separately from the actual development tool used to provide support for development, the IDE *is* the development tool. The modern OOIDE is usually tuned specifically to the development of Web-based integrated and distributed e-commerce solutions that are now at the core of IS development. IDEs provide support for the development project like traditional CASE tools did. They contain actual construction tools—for example, a programming language or some form of higher-level language—and they provide database connectivity and management facilities like traditional database management systems. They also provide for integration with existing applications and databases.

Some of the IDE tools have clearly evolved from the CASE world, some from the programming world, and some from the database world. For some of the tools, the integration is more complete and the origins difficult to discern. Regardless of origin, this type of tool brings together the types of functionality you previously would have had to use separate tools to obtain. You can expect this type of tool to evolve further and cover all or most of the needs for object-oriented system development. Some examples of this type of tool include Microsoft's Visual Studio, Computer Associate's Jasmine *ii*, IBM's VisualAge, Rational's Rational Suite, and Oracle's JDeveloper (or Internet Developer Suite).

Beyond the Basic Categories

Any attempt to categorize tools and technologies will rapidly become out of date. The successful products evolve and change. They adopt and adapt functionality from other successful types of tools. Through new development and mergers and acquisitions, products are integrated and developed to provide functionality way beyond what we have been used to. As products evolve, or as new tools are developed, new terms are needed to categorize and distinguish between them.

Vendors also want to associate their product, with or disassociate it from, certain product categories, depending on what is presently in fashion. The labeling of tools and the meaning of those labels are thus bound to change as the field evolves.

The Future of OO Tools

Expect to see a lot of development in the OO tools area. New categories of tools that we have not even thought of yet will emerge. New tools will appear and be touted as the best thing available to the OO developer, but some of them will never really make it in the marketplace. Others will provide functionality that we have not even conceived of yet and will shape the approach to IS development in the future. There will be a lot of new niche, or special-purpose, tools coming out. The IDEs will also become more powerful, partially by copying innovative new functionality from the niche products. On the commercial side there are presently a lot of players. There will, however, most likely be some sort of market shakeout, and we will eventually see a few major tool providers with tools that establish themselves as de facto standards. There will be a lot of mergers and acquisitions, and some of the tools you see today might well reappear under different names or as part of other tools.

On the technical side, there will be a steady development of new capabilities and functionality. At present, a lot of the development is Java-related in some way. One good way of keeping track of what is happening in the tools area is to read the current trade magazines. The *Java Developers Journal* (http://www.JavaDevelopersJournal.com/) is one of the major ones, and provides an annual readers' choice award, which will give you a good indication of what are the most popular tools in the industry.

The Web is also a good source of information, and there are a number of sites that provide information on object-oriented tools and technology. One example of a portal for links to information on object-oriented technology is www.cetus-links.org.

Key Terms

C#
C++
CASE
ICASE

Integrated Development
    Environment (IDE)
Java
Object-Oriented COBOL

persistent objects
Round trip engineering
Smalltalk

Review Questions

1. What is a pure object-oriented language versus a hybrid language?

2. What are two of the leading object-oriented languages in use? Which is a pure language and which is a hybrid language?

3. Describe some of the characteristics of C++.

4. Describe some of the characteristics of Java.

5. Why would object-oriented COBOL be of great interest to information system developers?

6. What are persistent objects and why are they particularly important for information systems?

7. What is an object-oriented database management system (OODBMS)?

8. What are the three ways that database management systems can handle persistent objects?

9. What is a CASE tool, and what is the difference between upper CASE and lower CASE tools?

10. What functionality should an IDE tool for object-oriented development provide for the developer?

Discussion Question

1. Object-oriented technology has been used successfully for years, primarily for control systems, graphical interfaces, operating environments, computer-aided design/computer graphics, and document-oriented systems. But is the technology really ready for developers of organizational information systems?

■ Exercises

1. Create a generalization/specialization hierarchy for types of programming languages, including object-oriented languages.

2. What do you think an object-oriented CASE tool should contain? Create a whole-part hierarchy to define your answer.

3. Create a generalization/specialization hierarchy to define the types of CASE tools. Would multiple inheritance apply here?

4. Look up the home pages for some of the OOIDE providers and try to describe and contrast various IDEs—for example, Computer Associate's Jasmine *ii*, Microsoft's Visual Studio, IBM's VisualAge, Rational's Rational Suite, or Oracle's JDeveloper (or Internet Developer Suite).

Java Code Examples Showing Problem Domain Classes

12

Introduction

Although object-oriented programming and implementation are beyond the scope of this book, it might be useful to see how some of the concepts are implemented in code. In other words, most information system developers want to know how object-oriented applications actually look. In object-oriented programming books it is not easy to find programming examples that apply to business information systems. Instead, the examples tend to emphasize applets that draw graphic objects on the screen or make use of utility classes included in class libraries that come with the programming language.

This chapter briefly introduces the Java programming language syntax and then explains how Java is used to create problem domain classes like the ones emphasized in this book. Object-oriented concepts are emphasized in the examples, and they are kept simple by implementing problem domain classes only. The programmer would actually start this way—from the middle out—beginning with the basic features of some of the problem domain classes in the use cases addressed in the first iteration of the project.

The key concepts shown include *classes, objects, attributes, methods, encapsulation, messages, inheritance, polymorphism,* and *association relationships.* Hopefully these concepts are familiar to you by now. Seeing how they are implemented in Java should help reinforce the concepts.

Java Program Syntax

Java is based on the C language syntax, so it should look familiar to C and C++ programmers. Unfortunately, Visual Basic and COBOL programmers find it quite different at first. A few simple rules help to clarify the syntax: First, Java is case sensitive, so uppercase and lowercase make a difference. For example, a variable named `John` is different from a variable named `john`, and the keyword `if` is valid but `If` is not. Each Java statement ends with a semicolon, but statements can continue from line to line without a continuation character. Each block of code is enclosed within curly braces `{ }`. Blocks of code are nested within each other, meaning that curly braces must be carefully placed to balance out. Two slashes indicate the beginning of a comment that extends to the end of the line.

Figure 12.1 shows a block of code. It begins with a curly brace. The first statement assigns a value to a variable and ends with a semicolon. The second statement also assigns a value to a variable, but it extends over two lines. Next is a nested block of code beginning with a curly brace. Another variable is assigned a value in the nested block. Then the nested block is closed by a curly brace. There is one final close curly brace for the whole block. Note that the nested block in this case doesn't serve any purpose other than to show the syntax. Note also that the curly braces can go anywhere on the page—there are no compiler rules about indenting or line spacing, but there are several style guidelines for indenting and arranging the statements for readability. The examples in this text follow a guideline that is useful when first learning Java. Experienced programmers tend to pack more statements onto a page.

```
{
        variable1 = "hello ";
        variable2 =
                    "world ";
        {variable3 = "example as you expect ";}
}
```

Figure 12.1 A block of Java code

Java provides standard programming constructs, including if...then...else, do...while, do...until, for, and standard numeric operations. Figure 12.2 shows some examples. The examples in this chapter do not use many of these constructs, but methods of problem domain classes would be written using them.

```
boolean x;
String y;
int z;

if (x = true)
{
        y = "hello world";
}
else
{
        y= "hello continent";
}

while (z < 10)
{
        z = z + 1;
}

for (int i; i<5; ++i)
{
        z = z - 1;
}
```

Figure 12.2 Some Java programming constructs

C-like operations that are commonly used include the increment/decrement numeric operators, and many information systems developers are not familiar with them. If there is a numeric variable `myNumber`, the statement `++myNumber` will add one to it (increment). Similarly, `--myNumber` will subtract one (decrement). There are lots of coding tricks and conventions used by programmers that sometimes make reading the code difficult.

Class Structure

In Java, each "program" must be a class that can have attributes and methods. Generally, one source code file is created for each class, with the filename the same as the class name and with the file extension of `java`. So, the source code for a class named Person is `Person.java`. When the file is compiled, it is named `Person.class`.

Figure 12.3 shows a simple example of the Person class introduced in Chapter 7. Internal documentation is included at the top of the file as comments beginning with two slashes. The first line in the example declares the name of the class: `public class Person`. The keyword `public` means that objects of the class can be accessed by anything in the system. Names of classes are capitalized by convention. After the class name, there is a begin curly brace to indicate that everything inside the block belongs to the class. The end curly brace at the bottom of the file ends the class.

Attributes of the Person class are declared next: `name` and `dateOfBirth`. These are simply variables declared in the class. By convention, attributes (and other variables) begin with a lowercase letter, and each additional word in the name is capitalized as shown. The keyword `private` means that no other object can directly access the value of the attribute or even find out its internal name. Only methods of the class can access or change the value. This enforces encapsulation and information hiding. The word `String` declares the data type of the attribute. It is capitalized because a String is actually a class (a collection of characters). Other data types are not capitalized: `int`, `single`, `double`, `byte`, `char`, etc.

A **constructor** is a special method used to create a new object of the class. The constructor name is the same as the class name. In order to create a new Person object, it is necessary to know the signature of the constructor, meaning the name and the arguments required to be passed to the constructor. In this case, the arguments include two strings, one for the name and one for the date of birth. If no constructor is included for the class, a default constructor is inherited that includes no arguments.

Following the constructor signature is a block of code with a begin curly brace and an end curly brace. This block is the programmer-supplied code executed when a new object is first created. Initial values are assigned to the two attributes in this example.

```
//
// Person, a problem domain class
//
public class Person
{
    //problem domain attributes of Person
    private String name;
    private String dateOfBirth;

    //constructor
    public Person(String aName, String aDate)
    {
       name = aName;
       dateOfBirth = aDate;
    }

    //standard methods
    public void setName(String aName)
    {
       name = aName;
    }
    public String getName()
    {
       return name;
    }
    public void setDateOfBirth(String aDate)
    {
       dateOfBirth = aDate;
    }
    public String getDateOfBirth()
    {
       return dateOfBirth;
    }
}
```

Figure 12.3   The Person class source code—`Person.java`

Next are methods of the class. The comment in the example labels them standard methods, although these methods are often called **accessor methods** because they allow access to the attributes of the class. By convention, accessor methods that set the value of an attribute begin with the word `set`, as in `setName` and `setDateOfBirth`. Methods that get the value of an attribute begin with `get`, as in `getName` and `getDateOfBirth`. Method names by convention begin with a lowercase letter. Note that the attributes are private, but if you want to know the value of an attribute, you can invoke the accessor method that gets it for you. The `set` methods can include validation procedures that protect the object's data, so encapsulation or information hiding is enforced by making attributes private but methods public.

The method begins with the access type (private or public), followed by a return type, the method name, and any arguments passed to the method. The return type indicates the type of data that is returned by the method. Get methods return the value of an attribute, for example, but usually do not accept an argument, so the method signature for `getName` is `public String getName()` because the method returns a String. Set methods usually do not return a value, but they do require an argument representing the new value for the attribute. When a method does not return a value, its return type is `void`. The method signature for `setName` is `public void setName(String aName)`.

The statements executed when the method is invoked are included in a block of code immediately after the method signature. The `set` methods in the example simply assign a new value to an attribute. No validation is included here. The get methods use the keyword `return` to indicate that they should return the value to the object that requested it. The statement `return name` indicates that the value of the name attribute is returned.

Once the problem domain code is written, it is compiled into a class file. Java classes are actually compiled into bytecode that can be executed on any platform that has a Java Virtual Machine installed. Therefore, the class file can be used without recompiling to create Person objects on a Windows PC, a Macintosh, an MVS mainframe, or a UNIX box. Device independence is an important benefit of Java for Internet applications.

■ Sending Messages in Driver Programs

New classes must be tested. It is important to remember that the class does not "run" like a procedural program. It defines the attributes and methods of a class—it is like a cookie cutter that is used to stamp out objects. One way to test classes is to create a **driver program** that creates objects of the class and sends messages to the objects. The concept is the same as a driver program in structured design, where a dummy module is created to test program modules. But the driver program used to test classes is a collection of messages sent one after the other.

Figure 12.4 shows a series of messages included in a driver program (complete examples of drivers are shown later in the chapter). The portion of the first statement after the equals sign asks the Person class to create a new person with the name of "Brian" and the date of birth of "July 28"—`new Person("Brian", "July 28")`. The `new` keyword invokes the **constructor** of the class, the two Strings are supplied to the constructor, the constructor creates a new Person object, and the statements in the constructor assign the two Strings to the attributes of the new object. An object of the Person class now exists in memory. It has a unique identity and it can be sent messages, just as we have described in this book.

```
//create two person objects

Person person1 = new Person("Brian", "July 28");
Person person2 = new Person("Kevin", "July 7");

//ask each person for its name and birth date
//and print the returned data to the screen

System.out.println(
        person1.getName() + person1.getDateOfBirth() +
        person2.getName() + person2.getDateOfBirth());
```

Figure 12.4   Messages sent to the Person class and to Person objects in a driver program

The first part of the statement, `Person person1`, declares a variable that the driver program can assign as a reference to the new object to use as an "address" for messages. The object reference is created by the constructor and then returned to the object requesting that the object be created, in this case, the driver program. When the driver program receives the object reference, it assigns it to the variable named `person1`. A Person reference can only be assigned to a variable declared as a Person, much as a String can only be assigned to a variable declared as a String. That is why the complete statement begins by declaring a variable and then asking that a new object be created with the returned object reference assigned to the variable.

The second line asks the Person class to create a second Person object with the name of "Kevin" and birth date of "July 7." The reference to the second object is assigned to the variable named `person2`.

Now that two objects exist in memory, the driver program can ask them for their names and birth dates. This tests two of the Person class methods and confirms that the constructor works correctly. The statement `System.out.println` tells the computer to display what is included in the parentheses to the system default output device (the screen).

The statement `person1.getName()` is a message to the object referenced by the variable `person1`. The object is `person1` and the message is `getName()`. Note that the message corresponds to the method name, so objects are able to receive messages only if they have a method that matches the message. The statement `person1.getDateOfBirth()` is another message to the person1 object. The plus sign between messages means that the strings returned by each message should be concatenated into one string.

The next line sends messages to the second person object, again asking for its name and date of birth. The string values returned are concatenated to make one long string. Remember that there are two separate objects here, each responds separately to messages. In other words, any Person object knows its name and date of birth, can supply these values when asked, and as we will see below, can change its name and data of birth when asked.

Once the four strings are returned and concatenated into one string, the `System.out.println` statement displays it on the screen. The output produced would be this:

```
BrianJuly 28KevinJuly 7
```

The driver program can also test the **set** methods, asking each Person object to change values assigned to its attributes. Figure 12.5 asks **person1** to set its name to "Ida" using the statement **person1.setName("Ida")**. The statement **person1.setDateOfBirth("January 29")** changes its date of birth. Note that the object's identity and object reference have not changed, but the values of its attributes have changed. The `System.out.println` statement displays the names and birth dates of both objects again, and this time the output looks like this:

```
IdaJanuary 29KevinJuly 7
```

Note that these two objects exist as long as the driver program is running, which is just for an instant. If a Java application or applet created these objects, they would exist in memory as long as the application or applet was running. For them to exist beyond that, it would be necessary to store the new objects in a file or database, as discussed in Chapter 11.

```
//continuation of the driver program from Figure 12.4
//ask person1 to change its name and birth date

person1.setName("Ida");
person1.setDateOfBirth("January 29");

//ask each person again for its name and birth date
//and print the returned data to the screen

System.out.println(
        person1.getName() + person1.getDateOfBirth() +
        person2.getName() + person2.getDateOfBirth());
```

Figure 12.5   Testing the `setName()` and `setDateOfBirth()` methods in a driver program

◼ Implementing Inheritance and Polymorphism

Now that we have one problem domain class, it is relatively easy to create a sub-class that inherits its attributes and methods. Recall the example in Chapter 7 that showed a Person class with subclasses for PatientPerson and DoctorPerson. Figure 12.6 shows the class diagram for the example. A PatientPerson has two additional attributes—an employer and an insurance company. A DoctorPerson also has two additional attributes—a date employed and a specialty.

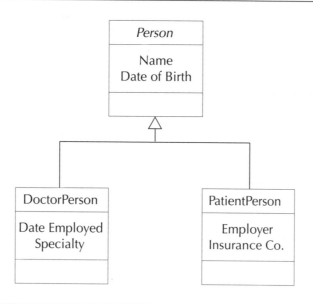

Figure 12.6   The Person generalization/specialization hierarchy with PatientPerson and DoctorPerson subclasses

The Java source code for the PatientPerson class is shown in Figure 12.7. To inherit, or extend, the Person class, it is only necessary to add the phrase `extends Person`, as in `public class PatientPerson extends Person`. Note that the attributes declared are the two additional attributes `employer` and `insuranceCompany`. It is not necessary to redeclare the attributes of Person. Similarly, the `get` and `set` methods included only apply to the additional attributes. When a PatientPerson object is created, it will automatically have all four attributes and all eight `get` and `set` methods.

```java
//
// PatientPerson
//
public class PatientPerson extends Person
{
    //problem domain attributes of PatientPerson
    //beyond those inherited from Person
    private String employer;
    private String insuranceCompany;

    //constructor
    public PatientPerson(String aName, String aDate,
                    String anEmployer, String anInsuranceCompany)
    {
      super(aName, aDate);
      employer=anEmployer;
      insuranceCompany = anInsuranceCompany;
    }

    //standard methods beyond those inherited from Person
    public void setEmployer(String anEmployer)
    {
      employer = anEmployer;
    }
    public String getEmployer()
    {
      return employer;
    }
    public void setInsuranceCompany(String anInsuranceCompany)
    {
      insuranceCompany = anInsuranceCompany;
    }
    public String getInsuranceCompany()
    {
      return insuranceCompany;
    }
    public String tellAboutSelf()
    {
      return "I am a Patient named " + getName() +
      " I was born " + getDateOfBirth() + "\n" +
      "  I work for " + getEmployer() +
      " and I am insured by " + getInsuranceCompany();
    }
}
```

Figure 12.7　The PatientPerson Class Source Code—`PatientPerson.java`

The constructor for PatientPerson expects four arguments—a name, a date, an employer, and an insurance company. The constructor then invokes the constructor of the Person class, the superclass, using the **super** keyword, followed by the two String arguments the Person constructor expects. All of the code in the Person class constructor is then executed. Then the additional statements in the PatientPerson constructor are executed. The result is that all four values are assigned to the attributes of the new PatientPerson.

Consider the power of this code. The programmer can "reuse" the Person class by extending it to make a new class. The programmer does not have to know anything about the internal structure of the Person class; indeed, she might not have the source code. All she needs to know is the signature of the constructor and the signatures of the methods. Then she puts the class to use.

There is an additional method included for PatientPerson—**tellAboutSelf()**. This method returns one string that includes details of the PatientPerson object. Note that string literals are concatenated with values returned by methods. More about this method below.

Figure 12.8 shows the source code for the other subclass—DoctorPerson. It also adds two attributes and four **get** and **set** methods, but they are different attributes and methods than those in the PatientPerson class. The constructor expects four strings as arguments, and the superclass constructor of Person is also invoked.

The **tellAboutSelf()** method in DoctorPerson has the same name as the method in PatientPerson, and note that the statements in both methods are similar. When a DoctorPerson is asked to tell about itself, it responds in its way, supplying information any DoctorPerson would know about itself. However, when a PatientPerson object is asked to tell about itself, it will answer as a PatientPerson would. This is an example of polymorphism, whereby two different types of objects respond in their own special way to the same message.

A complete driver program that tests the DoctorPerson and PatientPerson classes is shown in Figure 12.9. This is a class named PersonDriver, stored in a source code file named **PersonDriver.java**. Although it is technically a "class," it actually runs more like a procedural program. The method named **main(String args[])** is a static method, a method that belongs to the class rather than to objects of the class. The main method will run automatically like a program. Java applications start in this way, by including a class with a static main method.

Within the main method are messages like those shown in the driver code examples above. This driver first creates two DoctorPerson objects. Note that the object references **person1** and **person2** now refer more specifically to DoctorPerson objects. The call to the constructor includes all four string values expected by the DoctorPerson class.

Next, two PatientPersons are created, with **person3** and **person4** references specifically to PatientPerson objects. Now there are four objects in memory ready to respond to messages when asked.

```java
//
// DoctorPerson
//
public class DoctorPerson extends Person
{
    //problem domain attributes of DoctorPerson
    //beyond those inherited from Person
    private String dateEmployed;
    private String specialty;

    //constructor
    public DoctorPerson(String aName, String aDate,
          String aDateEmployed, String aSpecialty)
    {
      super(aName, aDate);
      dateEmployed = aDateEmployed;
      specialty = aSpecialty;
    }

    //standard methods beyond those inherited from Person
    public void setDateEmployed(String aDate)
    {
      dateEmployed = aDate;
    }
    public String getDateEmployed()
    {
      return dateEmployed;
    }
    public void setSpecialty(String aSpecialty)
    {
      specialty = aSpecialty;
    }
    public String getSpecialty()
    {
      return specialty;
    }
    public String tellAboutSelf()
    {
    return "I am a Doctor named " + getName() +
       " I was born " + getDateOfBirth() + "\n" +
       "  I was hired on " + getDateEmployed() +
       " and my specialty is " + getSpecialty();
    }
}
```

Figure 12.8   The DoctorPerson class source code—DoctorPerson.java

Within the `System.out.println` method, all four objects are asked to tell about themselves. Since both PatientPerson objects and DoctorPerson objects have a method named `tellAboutSelf()`, all four objects are able to respond. But they respond in their own way, with a doctor saying "I am a doctor with a specialty," and a patient saying "I am a patient with an insurance company." The output produced when the driver program runs is shown in Figure 12.10. Note that "\n" inserts a new line character into the string.

```
//
// PersonDriver - for testing problem domain classes
//
public class PersonDriver
{
    public static void main(String args[])
    {
      //create two DoctorPersons: person1 and person2
      DoctorPerson person1 = new DoctorPerson("John", "Feb 4",
                    "Sept 1", "internal medicine");
      DoctorPerson person2 = new DoctorPerson("JoAnn", "March 29",
                    "Jan 1", "general surgery");

      //create two PatientPersons: person3 and person4
      PatientPerson person3 = new PatientPerson("Brian", "July 28",
                    "Ajax Corporation", "Insurance of Omaha");
      PatientPerson person4 = new PatientPerson("Kevin", "July 7",
                    "Planet Video", "Travelers Insurance");

      //ask each person to tell us about itself
      System.out.println(
          person1.tellAboutSelf() + "\n" +
          person2.tellAboutSelf() + "\n" +
          person3.tellAboutSelf() + "\n" +
          person4.tellAboutSelf() + "\n");
    }
}
```

Figure 12.9   The PersonDriver program for testing the DoctorPerson and PatientPerson classes

Recall that the Person class in Chapter 7 is an abstract class—a class without objects. The "system" for the medical clinic is only interested in persons if they are either doctors or patients. To make the Person class abstract with Java, the keyword `abstract` is inserted before the class name. The driver program in Figure 12.10 would run the same either way. The code would look like this:

```
public abstract class Person
```

```
I am a Doctor named John I was born Feb 4
   I was hired on Sept 1 and my specialty is internal medicine
I am a Doctor named JoAnn I was born March 29
   I was hired on Jan 1 and my specialty is general surgery
I am a Patient named Brian I was born July 28
   I work for Ajax Corporation and I am insured by Insurance of Omaha
I am a Patient named Kevin I was born July 7
   I work for Planet Video and I am insured by Travelers Insurance
```

Figure 12.10   The output produced by the PersonDriver program

Implementing Association Relationships

The medical clinic example in Chapter 7 also included a Treatment class with an association between PatientPerson and Treatment. Each Treatment is associated with one PatientPerson, and each PatientPerson can have many Treatments. In Chapter 7, each Treatment was also associated with one DoctorPerson, but we have left that out of the class diagram shown in Figure 12.11 to keep the example simple.

Association relationships, like the one between Treatment and PatientPerson, are very common in business information systems. This section shows one way to implement them using Java. The basic idea is to include an attribute in each class to hold a reference to an object of the other class. This approach is quite different from the relational database approach, which uses foreign keys. The reference points to the actual object; it is not a foreign key.

The source code for the Treatment class is shown in Figure 12.12. Treatment does not inherit anything from another problem domain class. It has three problem domain attributes—`treatmentDate`, `startTime`, and `endTime`. What is different here is that a fourth attribute `patientPerson` is declared to hold a reference to an object of the PatientPerson class, declared as `private PatientPerson2 patientPerson`. `PatientPerson2` is a revised version of the PatientPerson class discussed below. Otherwise, the reference `patientPerson` is declared the same way as the object references in the driver programs. It can be assigned a reference to an object of the PatientPerson2 type. Therefore, a Treatment can be associated with or connected to a patient.

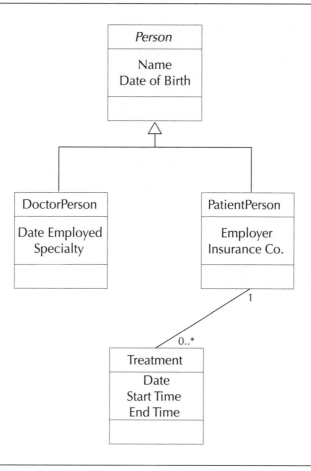

Figure 12.11 Class diagram for Clinic Showing Treatment class and association relationship with PatientPerson class

The constructor requires values for three attributes plus a reference to a PatientPerson object. Therefore, a treatment can only be created for an existing patient. This enforces the mandatory one-to-one relationship in the model. After creating the object, the constructor assigns the three values to the three attributes and then assigns the patient object reference to the `patientPerson` attribute.

```
//
// Treatment -- a problem domain class
//
public class Treatment
{
    //problem domain attributes of Treatment
    private String treatmentDate;
    private String startTime;
    private String endTime;

    //a reference to the PatientPerson2 associated with the Treatment
    //a mandatory association with cardinality/multiplicity of 1 to 1
    private PatientPerson2 patientPerson;

    //constructor
    public Treatment(String aDate, String time1,
                        String time2, PatientPerson2 aPatient)
    {
      treatmentDate = aDate;
      startTime = time1;
      endTime = time2;
      //assign the patient reference
      patientPerson = aPatient;
      //ask that patient to associate with this treatment
      patientPerson.associateWithTreatment(this);
    }

    //standard methods (no "set" methods included)
    public String getTreatmentDate()
    {
      return treatmentDate;
    }
    public String getStartTime()
    {
      return startTime;
    }
    public String getEndTime()
    {
      return endTime;
    }
}
```

Figure 12.12   The Treatment class source code—Treatment.java

The last statement in the constructor literally asks the PatientPerson object to associate with this new treatment, by sending the message patientPerson.associateWithTreatment(this). The PatientPerson2 class has a method with the signature associateWithTreatment (Treatment aTreatment), discussed below. The keyword this is a reference to the treatment being created. One problem domain object sends a message to another problem domain object of a different class, asking it to do something, which it does.

Standard get methods are included, but set methods are not shown in the example. If the designer wants to limit the ability to change attribute values, the set methods are left out.

The PatientPerson class has to be revised to allow it to associate with many treatments. Figure 12.13 shows the revised class, named PatientPerson2. It still inherits from Person, and it can be changed without affecting any other class.

```java
//
// PatientPerson2 -- enhanced to include an association with Treatment
//
public class PatientPerson2 extends Person
{
    //problem domain attributes of PatientPerson
    //beyond those inherited from Person
    private String employer;
    private String insuranceCompany;

    //a reference to an array of Treatments to represent the 1:n association
    //between PatientPerson2 and Treatments (cardinality/multiplicity is 1:n)
    private Treatment[] treatments;

    //count of treatments associated with this PatientPerson
    private int treatmentCount;

    //constructor
    public PatientPerson2(String aName, String aDate,
                    String anEmployer, String anInsuranceCompany)
    {
      super(aName, aDate);
      employer = anEmployer;
      insuranceCompany = anInsuranceCompany;
      //create the array to hold 10 treatment references and set count to 0
      treatments = new Treatment[10];
      treatmentCount = 0;
    }
```

(continued)

```java
//standard methods
public void associateWithTreatment(Treatment aTreatment)
{
  //add 1 to the counter and add the treatment reference to the array
   treatments[++treatmentCount] = aTreatment;
}
public String getAllTreatments()
{
  String allTreatments;
  allTreatments = "Treatments for Patient " + getName() + " include: \n";
  //for each treatment in the array, ask for its date and times
  //and concatenate to the string variable allTreatments
  for (int i=1; i<=treatmentCount; i++)
  {
      allTreatments = allTreatments + "  Treatment " + i +
         " dated " + treatments[i].getTreatmentDate() +
         " started at " + treatments[i].getStartTime() +
         " and ended at " + treatments[i].getEndTime() + "\n";
  }
  return allTreatments;
}
public void setEmployer(String anEmployer)
{
  employer = anEmployer;
}
public String getEmployer()
{
  return employer;
}
public void setInsuranceCompany(String anInsuranceCompany)
{
  insuranceCompany = anInsuranceCompany;
}
public String getInsuranceCompany()
{
  return insuranceCompany;
}
public String tellAboutSelf()
{
  return "I am a Patient named " + getName() +
  " I was born " + getDateOfBirth() + "\n" +
  "  I work for " + getEmployer() +
  " and I am insured by " + getInsuranceCompany();
}
}
```

Figure 12.13   The revised PatientPerson class with references to treatments—
                  `PatientPerson2.java`

Since the association between PatientPerson and Treatment is one to many, it is more complicated to code. First, instead of having one reference to a Treatment, there must be many references to Treatments. Usually the programmer will use a special collection class, such as a Vector, to hold a collection of references. In this example, a simple array with subscripts is used.

The array named `treatments` will contain object references of the Treatment class, declared as `private Treatment[] treatments`. Recall that relational database theory states that first normal form requires only one value for each attribute of a data entity. That is not always the case with object-oriented programming as the array with many treatment references indicates. Because an fact that the array is used to hold object references, a counter named `treatmentCount` is declared as an index for the array.

The expanded constructor adds statements to create the actual array of up to ten Treatment references (`treatments = new Treatment[10]`) and to initialize `treatmentCount` to zero. Note that the PatientPerson can be created without requiring an associated treatment because cardinality/multiplicity is zero or more treatments (optional).

A standard method named `associateWithTreatment` is added for PatientPerson as discussed above. This method is invoked when a new Treatment sends a message to the PatientPerson. The argument expected by the method is a reference to a Treatment object. The single statement in the method first adds one to the counter (as `++treatmentCount` using the increment operator) and then assigns the value of the Treatment object reference to the next position in the treatments array.

A sequence diagram shown in Figure 12.14 documents a scenario in which the user asks a PatientPerson to get information about all of its Treatments. To implement this scenario, an additional method named `getAllTreatments` is added to the PatientPerson2 class. This method goes through each treatment reference in the array and asks each referenced object for information about its date, startTime, and endTime. A `for` loop is used in this example (there are notations that can be used on the sequence diagram to indicate repetition if desired). Note that the method names in the classes are the same as the message names on the sequence diagram. So messages from one problem domain object (a PatientPerson) go to many different Treatment objects when the method is invoked. Information from all of the associated Treatment objects is combined into one string, `allTreatments`, which is declared locally in the method, and then the string is returned to the user, just as in the sequence diagram.

A driver program to test the Treatment class and the expanded PatientPerson2 class is shown in Figure 12.15. First, three PatientPerson2 objects are created, Brian, Kevin, and Ida. Next, seven Treatment objects are created. Note that the new treatments are not assigned to object references in the driver program. But the constructor requires that each treatment be given a reference to a PatientPerson object, in this case, **person1**, **person2**, or **person3**. Therefore, the first treatment is on August 4th, starting at 1:00, ending at 1:20, for the object referenced by **person1**. The constructor of Treatment asks the PatientPerson to associate with the Treatment, so we can find the treatment by asking the patient about it. Methods could be added to Treatment to get all patient information as well.

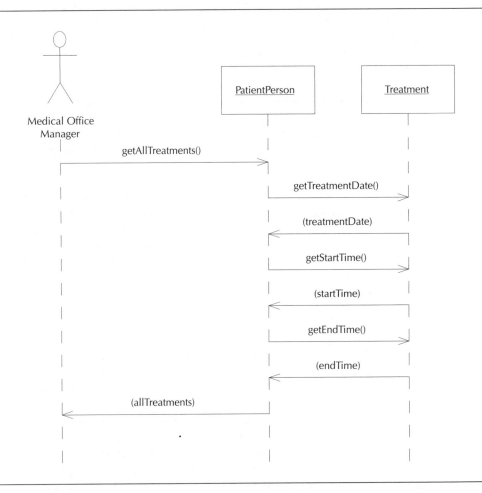

Figure 12.14   Sequence diagram showing object interactions when a user asks a PatientPerson object to get all treatments

After the three paients and seven treatments are created, the driver program asks each person to **tellAboutSelf()**. Then each person is asked to **getAllTreatments()**. The output produced is shown in Figure 12.16. Again, the objects exist in memory only for an instant as the driver program is running, but in a finished application they would exist and respond to messages as long as needed.

```java
//
// PersonDriver2 — for testing problem domain classes
//
public class PersonDriver2
{
    public static void main(String args[])
    {
      //create three PatientPersons: person1, person2, and person3
      PatientPerson2 person1 = new PatientPerson2("Brian", "July 28",
                    "Ajax Corporation", "Insurance of Omaha");
      PatientPerson2 person2 = new PatientPerson2("Kevin", "July 7",
                    "Planet Video", "Travelers Insurance");
      PatientPerson2 person3 = new PatientPerson2("Ida", "January 29",
                    "Agder University", "National Plan");

      //create Treatments for PatientPersons (no references needed by driver)
      new Treatment("August 4",  "1:00",  "1:20",  person1);
      new Treatment("August 6",  "3:00",  "3:15",  person1);
      new Treatment("August 10", "10:00", "11:20", person1);
      new Treatment("August 15", "1:00",  "1:35",  person2);
      new Treatment("August 18", "9:00",  "9:45",  person2);
      new Treatment("August 21", "4:00",  "4:20",  person3);
      new Treatment("August 28", "8:30",  "9:15",  person3);

      //ask each person to tell us about itself
      System.out.println(
          person1.tellAboutSelf() + "\n" +
          person2.tellAboutSelf() + "\n" +
          person3.tellAboutSelf() + "\n");

      //ask each PatientPerson for all of its treatments
      System.out.println(
          person1.getAllTreatments() + "\n" +
          person2.getAllTreatments() + "\n" +
          person3.getAllTreatments() + "\n");
    }
}
```

Figure 12.15 The PersonDriver2 program for testing treatment and PatientPerson associations

```
I am a Patient named Brian I was born July 28
  I work for Ajax Corporation and I am insured by Insurance of Omaha
I am a Patient named Kevin I was born July 7
  I work for Planet Video and I am insured by Travelers Insurance
I am a Patient named Ida I was born January 29
  I work for Agder University and I am insured by National Plan

Treatments for Patient Brian include:
  Treatment 1 dated August 4 started at 1:00 and ended at 1:20
  Treatment 2 dated August 6 started at 3:00 and ended at 3:15
  Treatment 3 dated August 10 started at 10:00 and ended at 11:20

Treatments for Patient Kevin include:
  Treatment 1 dated August 15 started at 1:00 and ended at 1:35
  Treatment 2 dated August 18 started at 9:00 and ended at 9:45

Treatments for Patient Ida include:
  Treatment 1 dated August 21 started at 4:00 and ended at 4:20
  Treatment 2 dated August 28 started at 8:30 and ended at 9:15
```

Figure 12.16   Output produced by the PersonDriver2 program

These Java problem domain class examples are simplified in a number of ways. No validation or error handling is included, for example. Additionally, no user interface classes are included, and there is no provision for making the objects persistent (i.e., no database management capability is included). Hopefully, the examples help show how object-oriented programming is used to implement the key object-oriented concepts.

■ Key Terms

abstract	driver program	single
accessor methods	extends	string
byte	int	super
char	private	this
constructor	public	void
double	return	

Review Questions

1. What language is Java based on?

2. What does it mean for a language like Java to be case sensitive?

3. What symbols are used to define a block of Java code?

4. What symbol is used to define the end of a Java statement?

5. What symbols are used to define a one-line comment in Java?

6. Show an example of a statement that adds 1 to a variable named myNumber using the Java increment operator. Write an equivalent statement that does not use the increment operator.

7. What file extension does a Java source code file have? What extension does the compiled bytecode file have?

8. What does public access to a class or method allow?

9. Why give private access to attributes?

10. Why is String capitalized but single and double are not capitalized?

11. What is a constructor?

12. What are two types of accessor methods?

13. What would be the return type of a method that returns the price of a product in dollars?

14. What is a driver program, and what kind of "statements" does it contain?

15. The extends keyword allows what OO concept in Java?

16. The abstract keyword allows what OO concept in Java?

17. Explain how association relationships are implemented with Java.

Discussion Questions

1. Java uses structured programming constructs, as shown in Figure 12.2. Explain where the object-oriented approach uses structured programming.

2. Java is used in this chapter to show how problem domain classes are created. User interface classes, on the other hand, come predefined in class libraries. Therefore, GUI programming involves using the predefined classes rather than creating classes from scratch. Discuss.

3. What are some implications of using an array of object references to establish a one-to-many relationship between PatientPerson and Treatment and of using foreign keys in a relational database?

■ Exercises

1. Write Java code to define the second VideoItem class in Chapter 6, the one with the recordViewing method. Write a Java driver program to test the class by creating several Video objects, recording several viewings of each one, and then displaying the date last viewed and number of viewings.

2. Write Java code to define the two class examples of Video and VideoItem, including the association relationship between them. Write a Java driver program to test the classes.

3. Consider the problem domain classes in the Dick's Dive 'n' Thrive case. Write Java code to define and test the following sets of classes, considering each set separately:
   - Customer, Contract, and ContractItem (standard methods only)
   - The complete BoatAssembly
   - The complete RentalEquipment generalization/specialization hierarchy including the Boat Assembly

4. Try completing more of the system by modifying ContractItem and RentalEquipment to allow the association relationship. Write a driver to test the revised classes. Add the custom methods to Contract and ContractItem and test them.

Moving to Object-Oriented Development: Why and How

13

Introduction

Why move to the object-oriented approach? What are the possible benefits of using object-oriented development? What is the best way to manage the shift from traditional to object-oriented development so that these benefits are achieved? This chapter takes a closer look at these issues.

The object-oriented approach is a different way to develop systems. Some claim that the object-oriented approach implies a paradigm shift, a different way of viewing the world (of system development). Such a shift is likely to lead to problems and have its pitfalls. In this chapter, we also discuss some of the dark clouds that might be gathering on the horizon.

Some problems from the shift result from the transition from traditional system development to object-oriented development. This transition can be a major undertaking, one that requires a great commitment of resources. We will briefly discuss some of the managerial challenges related to this transition. Understanding these challenges should also help you decide how to move forward in your own career, and we will conclude with some considerations about this.

The Benefits of Object-Oriented Development

The notion that there is a software crisis is widespread. The productivity for software development has not increased substantially over the years. Some research suggests there has been less than a 10-fold increase since the early sixties. The information system projects now in the pipeline tend to be larger and more complex than previous projects. There is a growing need for rapid delivery of software to support businesses in an increasingly competitive world. Time to market is often of paramount importance for systems developed for modern Web-centric and e-commerce-oriented applications. The increase in productivity we have seen over the years has not kept pace with the increase in demand for speedy delivery of new software. This is a serious problem by itself, but it is compounded by the fact that existing software systems require a massive maintenance effort to keep them operable. It is estimated that some companies spend as much as 80% of their potential development resources for maintenance. There are four main reasons for the maintenance requirements:

1. Specifying and programming software systems is a very complicated undertaking. Logical and syntactical code errors will usually occur.

2. Requirements specification is a major challenge in systems development. Often the specified requirements do not reflect the users' real needs, and these needs are not even clear to the users until after the first version of the software is running.

3. Additional features that could not be accommodated in the original development might be needed.

4. The business environment that the software is supporting might be changing.

All four points lead to changes in existing software; these changes are usually called maintenance. Those related to items 3 and 4 should more correctly be called enhancements or extensions. Those related to items 1 and 2 are maintenance in a more correct sense of the word.

To eliminate the software crisis, we will have to learn to build quality software faster and in a way that facilitates enhancements and change. We will briefly discuss how object-oriented system development conceivably will address the problems with productivity, maintainability, and extendibility.

Productivity

From a programming perspective, there are many problems that a traditional functional language does not lend itself to solving easily. Development of graphical user interfaces (GUI) and simulation applications are some examples. In most cases, the use of object-oriented languages tends to result in shorter and more compact and efficient code. This might in itself enhance productivity somewhat.

Far more important is the opportunity for reuse. Object-orientation allows a building-block approach to system development—assembling applications partially by using existing, pretested classes found in class libraries and partially by packaging (parts of) software as packages or components that can be incorporated in other systems. If these features are exploited properly, a significant increase in productivity is likely to occur. This is usually hailed as one of the main advantages of the object-oriented approach.

Maintainability and Quality

Improved maintainability is also cited as one of the main advantages of the object-oriented approach. The maintenance problem is alleviated both by reducing the need for corrections through development of better-quality systems, and by making it easier to make any changes that are eventually needed.

Logical and syntactical errors. Object-oriented software is constructed using self-contained object classes. Objects tend to be small in terms of the number of programming statements that are needed to implement them. This leads to small manageable units within the system, reducing the overall complexity of the software. Less complexity means fewer errors.

By using preexisting, pretested object classes as the building blocks for new systems, the amount of new code is reduced. Less new code means fewer errors.

Errors will still occur, but corrections can be made to the interior structure or processing rules of the object class without creating unforeseen changes throughout the system. Because of the compact size and independence of classes, it is relatively easy, even for persons without updated documentation or intimate knowledge of the system, to get the overview and understanding necessary to do the corrections.

Missing or incorrect specifications. Specifications define what to build. The ability to build systems according to the specifications is required in system development. However, it is not enough to build right, with efficiency and without errors. We must also build the right things. Many of the problems with information systems are related to a poor understanding of what the users actually need. This leads to missing or incorrect specifications, which again lead to low-quality systems. Object-oriented development addresses this problem in several ways.

Most traditional information systems were developed using some variation of a structured development approach whereby the most common modeling techniques used were data flow diagramming and data modeling. These techniques are not well suited for communicating with users about system functionality. They force users into an abstract way of thinking, quite far removed from the way they usually think about their work. Dealing with system objects that closely resemble real-life objects is more natural for users than dealing with entities, relationships, and data flows. So the object-oriented development approach promises to narrow the communication gap by using modeling concepts and techniques that are more closely related to the users' way of thinking. Object-orientation also facilitates a prototyping approach, which further narrows the communication gap and enhances the understanding of the real requirements.

Traditionally, it has been necessary to employ multiple modeling techniques to capture all the detail as the developers move through the life cycle phases. This is best exemplified by the transformation from data flow diagrams to program structure charts as we move from structured analysis to structured design. Such transformations are cumbersome and error prone. Information conveyed in one model might not be retained in the next or inconsistencies between the models might easily occur. Object models allow us to remain in the same modeling context for the duration of the project, thereby also increasing the quality of the development effort.

Extendibility

A system will eventually need to be changed either because all of the required functionality was not originally included in the system or because the business need for the system has changed.

Adding features. With the object-oriented approach, methods and attributes can be added to existing object classes without disrupting the rest of the system. New classes can also be added easily. By exploiting the inheritance feature, these tasks can usually be accomplished with little programming effort.

The expedience with which new features can be added facilitates an evolutionary or incremental approach to system development. The main functionality can be made available for the user quickly, and additional features can be added when time allows.

Accommodating business changes. In a competitive world, it is of paramount importance that the information systems accommodate the changes in the business environment. Such changes are clearly occurring at an increasing rate. Because of the self-contained nature of the object classes and the inheritance feature, object-oriented systems are much easier to change and expand than traditional systems.

It can be seen from the discussion above that an object-oriented approach conceivably can address all the main underlying reasons for the software crisis. This approach is not, however, the magical silver bullet that will solve all the problems with information systems. Information system development is an inherently complex task, and it will continue to be so. As our ability to cope with system development complexity increases, so will the tendency to take on ever more complex projects.

Problems with the Object-Oriented Approach

The potential benefits of the object-oriented system development approach presented above are not automatically attainable. Using object-oriented technology, it is still possible to design and program truly awful software in terms of quality and maintainability.

As mentioned before, object-oriented technologies and development methods are still not mature or stable. Object-oriented development will remain leading edge for some time, with all the potential problems inherent in such a situation.

Any large-scale change to new technology and methods is likely to be time-consuming. Experience with new technology, such as CASE and comprehensive development methodologies, indicates that there is a substantial learning curve effect. Productivity and quality decrease as staff are learning new methods and tools. This learning period might be as long as a 6 to 12 months. Switching to an object-oriented approach and object-oriented tools will probably pose even larger challenges for the staff, and similar or longer learning periods are to be expected.

Some of the benefits of the object-oriented approach will only show up after a considerable length of time. If less resources are needed for maintenance and enhancements, this will only be evident some time after the system is in use. The more time that elapses, the larger the savings are likely to be.

Benefits from reuse are mainly achievable after a certain portfolio of systems has been developed (although some reuse might be achieved with standard class libraries).

It should be evident then that if management is looking for quick fixes and short-term return on investment, object-oriented development efforts might easily be considered failures and the methods and tools shelved.

Introducing an object-oriented development approach will, in most cases, mean a major change in thinking patterns and work habits for those involved. Such changes can hardly be implemented successfully without a major commitment of time and resources. Taken on lightly, an attempt to switch to object-oriented development might create more problems than it solves.

Changing to the Object-Oriented Approach

As already mentioned, switching to an object-oriented methodology will usually be a major undertaking, and some general guidelines for managing the change can be provided. The change effort should be organized as a project. It should be planned and scheduled, performance goals and criteria need to be established, resources need to be estimated and allocated, roles and responsibilities need to be clearly spelled out, and the project must be managed and controlled like any other development project. Expectations need to be realistic, and a long-term commitment from management is crucial.

Generally, there are three different areas that need to be considered when changing to the object-oriented approach. These are:

1. **Tools**
   The right programming environment, database, and CASE tool need to be selected and implemented.

2. **Methodology**
   The right methodology has to be selected and implemented.

3. **Organization**
   The necessary training must be provided. Organizational impact must be assessed. A suitable pilot project must be selected. The change effort must be planned and managed. And the right people must be available.

Failure in any of these three areas is likely to render the whole project a failure. The most important obstacles often seem to be those dealing with people: organizational issues and resistance to change.

The best way to get started is usually a pilot project approach. This will allow management to select good, motivated people and a project of suitable size and complexity. This is important to ensure a successful project. Success with the pilot project will pave the way for further change. Pilot project staff will become in-house specialists and resource persons, assisting other colleagues in their efforts to learn new methods and technologies.

The pilot project should be important and visible. The result should not be perceived as trivial. On the other hand, a totally new approach to system development is risky, and mission-critical projects should not be selected. Complexity and risk increase with size. It is important to keep the project size manageable and the likelihood of success as high as possible. The pilot project must be carefully measured and managed, and supported by management. Successes must be thoroughly advertised to increase interest and motivate colleagues to adopt the new tools and methods.

Both the organization and its members must be ready to accept and adjust to change. This readiness will have a major impact on the success of the project. Such readiness might be difficult to assess, but the software development maturity framework provided by Watts Humprey and the Software Engineering Institute (SEI) is a useful framework for thinking in these terms (Humprey 1989).

The software development maturity framework portrays software development organizations as advancing through different levels of maturity and capability, starting out on the initial level characterized by having a semichaotic or ad hoc development process. The framework also includes an instrument for assessing how mature an organization is. It provides detailed recommendations for moving from a less mature level to a more mature level.

It should be apparent from this brief presentation that introducing the object-oriented approach into an organization at an immature level will be quite different from doing the same thing in an organization at a more mature level. Introduction and establishment of any kind of system development methodology in an immature organization is usually a major effort requiring several years. Introducing object-oriented methodologies into such organizations might not be advisable, and will definitely be risky. The more mature an organization is, the less risky and the less time-consuming a change to object-oriented development is likely to be.

Regardless of maturity, a change to object-oriented development requires much more than learning new techniques and tools. The whole system development process will need to be altered, and a different mindset on the part of the developer is required. Even the potential benefits described earlier in the chapter have often not been sufficient to drive such a substantial change, and the adoption of object-oriented system development has been slower than many expected. The present focus on Web-centric e-commerce-oriented business applications is, however, a powerful factor in the adoption process and might well turn object-oriented technology into a competitive necessity for system developers

■ Preparing for Your Own Change to Object-Oriented Development

It should be evident from the discussion above that the change to an object-oriented approach is no trivial task. Difficult tasks require well-qualified people. The availability of such people is likely to be a main bottleneck as organizations move to the object-oriented approach. Because a fundamental change in their way of thinking is required of people trained in structured system development, young people with the right educational background might be able to compete successfully with more experienced information system developers.

This text has, we hope, helped you understand the object-oriented approach and appreciate its potential in the system development field. If you believe that the object-oriented approach will have a major impact and create a demand for people with training in object-oriented technology, you might contemplate positioning yourself to make the most of the potential demand.

So is now the right time for the information systems field in general and for you in particular to move to object-oriented development? We hope this book has provided some background to give you the necessary understanding to make that assessment. If you think that the world of object-orientation is exciting and you want to learn more about it, or if you are convinced that the object-oriented approach is upon us, we suggest you do something about it.

This book has just scratched the surface of the object-oriented approach. Read some of the books or look up some of the Web pages referred to in earlier chapters. The authors have a lot of experience using such methods, and they go into object-oriented development and issues about development in much greater depth than we have been able to do here.

If you have not yet started working with some of the object-oriented technology, start learning Java. Finally, whenever you think about a computer system, think of objects!

▌ Review Questions

1. What are the four main reasons that information systems require so much maintenance?

2. How might the object-oriented approach lead to greater system development productivity?

3. How might the object-oriented approach improve system maintainability and quality?

4. How might the object-oriented approach improve system extendibility?

5. What are some of the potential problems with the object-oriented approach?

Discussion Questions

1. Discuss whether the potential benefits of the object-oriented approach outweigh the potential risks.

2. To what extent do you think the object-oriented approach will have a major impact and create a demand for people with training in object-oriented technology?

3. Discuss whether you believe young people (without much traditional systems experience) have a potential advantage over more experienced people because of the shift to the object-oriented approach.

References

Cockburn, A. *Surviving Object Oriented Projects*. A Managers Guide. Reading, Massachusetts: Addison-Wesley, 1998.

Humprey, W. S. *Managing the Software Process*. Reading, Massachusetts: Addison-Wesley, 1989.

Index

F

features, adding with object-oriented approach, 199–200
flexibility, object-oriented approach, 9
formulas, 52

G

generalization relationships, 55
generalization/specialization hierarchies, 14, 46–47, 83–90
  associated with another class, 87–90
  identifying, 119–124
  with multiple inheritance, 92–93
graphical models, 52
graphical user interfaces (GUIs), 8, 19
  design, 145–155
  design enhancements to scenarios and sequence diagrams, 150–151
  overall system structure, 151–155
  three-tier design architecture, 143
groupware, 21
GUIs. *See* graphical user interfaces (GUIs)

H

hierarchies. *See* generalization/specialization hierarchies; whole-part hierarchies

I

ICASE (Integrated CASE), 165, 166–167
IDEs (Integrated Development Environments), 165, 167
implementation phase, system development life cycles, 102
include relationships, 55
incorrect specifications, 199
incremental development, 103
information hiding, 44
Ingres, 164
inheritance, 46–47
  Java language, 179–184
  multiple, 92–93
  requirements models, 90–91
Integrated CASE (ICASE), 165, 166–167
Integrated Development Environments (IDEs), 165, 167
Internet Developer Suite, 167
iterative approach, system development life cycles, 102

J

J++ language, 8
Jacobson, Ivar, 8
JAD (joint application design), 102, 103
Jasmine *ii*, 167
Java Developers Journal, 168

Java

Java language, 8, 159, 161, 164, 166
  association relationships, 185–193
  class structure, 174–176
  examples showing problem domain classes, 171–193
  inheritance and polymorphism, 179–184
  sending messages in driver programs, 176–178
  syntax, 172–174
JDeveloper, 167
joint application design (JAD), 102, 103

L

lifelines, 62–63
logical errors, 198–199

M

maintainability, object-oriented approach, 198–199
maintenance phase, system development life cycles, 102
mandatory relationships, 58
maximum cardinality/multiplicity relationships, 58
menu(s), 146–149
menu hierarchy, 153–155
messages, 45, 63, 73–78
message sending, 45
  driver programs, 176–178
method(s), 43–44, 175–176
  accessor, 175–176
  custom, 70–73
  definition, 104
  encapsulation, 44
  identifying, 132–134
methodologies, system development, 104–106
  object-oriented, need for, 105–106
method signatures, 45
minimum cardinality/multiplicity relationships, 58
missing specifications, 199
models, 51–53
modular programming, 5
multimedia objects, 21–23
multiple inheritance, 92–93
multiplicity, 42–43

N

narrative models, 52

O

object(s), 11–24
  classes, 17
  classes versus, 39–40
  computer system as collection of, 2
  in computer systems, 17–18